Walk in Dry Places

Walk in
Dry Places

MEL B.

HAZELDEN®

Hazelden
Center City. Minnesota 55012-0176
1-800-328-9000 (Toll Free U.S.,
Canada. and the Virgin Islands)
1-651-213-4000 (Outside the U.S. and Canada)
1-651-213-4590 (24-hour FAX)
http://www.hazelden.org (World Wide Web site on Internet)
©1996 by Hazelden Foundation

ISBN 978-1-56838-127-5

Book design by Will H. Powers
Cover design by David Spohn
Typesetting by Stanton Publication Services. Inc.

Hazelden, a national nonprofit organization founded in 1949, helps people reclaim their lives from the disease of addiction. Built on decades of knowledge and experience, Hazelden offers a comprehensive approach to addiction that addresses the full range of patient, family, and professional needs, including treatment and continuing care for youth and adults, research, higher learning, public education and advocacy, and publishing.

A life of recovery is lived "one day at a time." Hazelden publications, both educational and inspirational, support and strengthen lifelong recovery. In 1954, Hazelden published *Twenty-Four Hours a Day*, the first daily meditation book for recovering alcoholics, and Hazelden continues to publish works to inspire and guide individuals in treatment and recovery, and their loved ones. Professionals who work to prevent and treat addiction also turn to Hazelden for evidence-based curricula, informational materials, and videos for use in schools, treatment programs, and correctional programs.

Through published works, Hazelden extends the reach of hope, encouragement, help, and support to individuals, families, and communities affected by addiction and related issues.

For questions about Hazelden publications, please call **800-328-9000** or visit us online at **hazelden.org/bookstore.**

INTRODUCTION

There are many meditation books on the shelves; why add to the list? What can be said about recovery that hasn't already been expressed countless times?

Walk in Dry Places was written to address the daily concerns of the "established" recovering person—one who has been clean and sober for a year or more. While continuous sobriety is indispensable for personal growth and real serenity, most of us also have much to do in learning to live life on the terms that other human beings can accept. We may be more disadvantaged than others because we have to start by repairing damage created by years of drinking or drugging. But we have the advantage of a Twelve Step program that really works if it is practiced daily.

There may be bumps and hurdles along the way. In 1956, for example, after achieving my own sobriety in a Twelve Step program, I was devastated to learn that AA cofounder Bill W. had suffered from severe depression long after achieving sobriety. What did that say for AA sobriety, I wondered, if the very author of the Twelve Steps had faltered in his quest for true serenity?

As the years of my recovery stretched out, I watched older members whose examples had guided me drift away from the program or even relapse. For them, AA did not have staying power; they had veered from sobriety to find grim relief in the world of alcoholism, and some of them never made a second return from this living hell. What had gone so wrong that they would choose again the very demons they had once escaped?

Close at hand were other friends who complained that their sobriety was marred by depression, discord, resentment, and fear. I talked frequently about such issues at discussion meetings, always being careful to keep the focus on sobriety. Sometimes, I had the disturbing feeling that these people were questioning whether a sober life was really worth it.

They needed—just as we continuously need—assurance that things can and will get better if we persevere in the program. I would love to repeat one operative word at every AA meeting: Continue! Continue! Continue!

We're claiming too much if we say that any meditation book will give us the happiness and stability we seek. But the right thoughts, presented in daily messages, can give us the frame of mind we need to continue in the program. We can use our books to accumulate new ideas for sober and clean living. We can use them to reinforce ideas discussed at meetings and in other literature. It is my hope that *Walk in Dry Places* will contribute to that process for many recovering people.

In writing these daily meditations, I must also acknowledge a debt to Rich W., the author of *Twenty-Four Hours a Day*. I never met Rich, but my very first copy of *Twenty-Four Hours* was privately published in his home in Daytona Beach, Florida. It caught on fast in AA, and after Rich released the book to Hazelden, its readership climbed into the millions. There's good reason to say that Rich's little book is one of the most important pieces of literature ever prepared for recovering people—nearly as important as AA's Big Book or the *Twelve and Twelve*. It would be impossible to calculate the good that has come from Rich's legacy.

I hope you'll continue using *Twenty-Four Hours a Day* and other meditation books. May the thoughts expressed in *Walk in Dry Places* touch the same responsive chords of feeling that Rich W. reached with *Twenty-Four Hours*. And be assured that you have my prayers for your good as we walk together, in dry places, on the road to happy destiny.

—MEL B.

January

JANUARY 1

A YEAR TO GROW

Growth This new year can be a time of growth in sobriety. While we have no crystal ball that tells us what luck and fortune the year will bring, we do have a program that gives us the power to make the best of this year, to grow in sobriety. We can make progress in overcoming resentment and selfishness, we can help others in their search for happy sobriety, and we can make better use of our talents and opportunities.

We can live sober, and we also can find happiness and true self-esteem in sobriety. In our drinking, a desperate search for happiness and self-esteem compelled us to drink, but we could never find our happy destiny in the bottle. No matter what came to us, things had a way of turning sour as we continued to drink and to take other harmful substances.

In our new life, we have good reason to feel confident and optimistic. We have friends who understand us; we have sponsors who will share with us their own experience and hope. We have a Higher Power who is, as the poet Tennyson said, "closer to us than breathing, and nearer than hands and feet." We face nothing alone, and in the new year all experiences can help us grow.

I face this day with confidence, courage, and optimism. I will know that my Higher Power is present in every person and situation.

JANUARY 2

THE DELUSION OF "JUST ONE MORE"

Other Excesses A binge is a chain reaction that starts with one drink. After a grim period of enforced abstinence, that first drink may have brought us intense emotional release and a peak feeling of euphoria. For the rest of the binge, there was a continuing delusion that the next drink would help us recapture that peak experience.

Delusion leads us to other excesses. Some alcoholics also binge on smoking, food, sex, and power and recognition. In this frantic seeking, our basic delusion is that substances and things can satisfy what is really a spiritual need. Instead of realizing that there is a law of diminishing returns in the enjoyment of such things, we cling to the delusion that "just one more" will bring the relief and satisfaction we want.

Delusions brought disillusionment, and only the truth set us free from alcohol. Other excesses might not hurt us to the extent alcohol did, but the excesses of our drinking years carry lessons that are equally applicable to other human problems.

I will carry out the day's activities knowing that I already have enough of everything I need *for this day alone.*

JANUARY 3

FORGIVING OTHERS

Releasing the Past There is a general reluctance on the part of most people to forgive old injuries. Some of us wasted lots of time brooding about old wrongs done to us or trying to get even for some past injustice.

But the only way we can ever really get even is to forgive others completely and without the slightest hidden reservation. If we haven't forgiven others, the old resentments are a poison in our own lives. We continue to feel the pain of the original injury, and the ensuing resentment destroys our peace of mind and endangers our relationships.

In forgiving others, we do not grant a favor to them, but *to ourselves.* By extending forgiveness, we release thoughts and feelings that have been like a cancer in our lives. We are not giving up a possession or a right; instead, we are freeing ourselves from a burden that nobody needs to carry. We are letting go of garbage that we do not need in our lives. When we forgive others, we also realize that *we* are forgiven. As it is stated in closing meetings, "Forgive us our trespasses, as we forgive those who trespass against us."

I will not review past hurts and injuries this day. I will go through the day knowing that God forgives me to the extent that I forgive others.

GOD'S WILL FOR US

Higher Will   More than one alcoholic has trouble learning and accepting God's will. This difficulty may grow out of the old belief that God's will is going to be something unpleasant or dull. "I was afraid of learning God's will, because I thought I might have to go off to Africa as a missionary," one young person said at a meeting.

But God only intends what is best for us; therefore, the only real happiness and security comes from learning and carrying out God's will. God's plan is always better and greater than anything we might produce when depending solely on human reason. Our own view and understandings are limited, but God can see a breathtaking sweep of wonderful activities and opportunities for us.

Most of us, by yielding to self-will, lose out in the search for real joy, true success, and genuine happiness. Our alcoholism was perhaps the best example of self-will in action. It was only when we turned to a Higher Power that we began to find the things that we had been vainly seeking in the bottle. God has brought us this far and will not fail us when we ask for guidance and understanding in other matters.

I will keep in mind today that God's will for me is good, and that God gives me the power to live in peace and harmony with others.

JANUARY 5

THE PROBLEM OF GOSSIP

Breaking Free from Faults   Our character defects hang on tenaciously because we secretly enjoy or need them. Gossip is an example of this problem. Most of us know that gossip is mean and malicious, yet we enjoy the spurious self-satisfaction and self-importance it gives us.

However, this feeling of self-satisfaction and self-importance is fleeting. When we engage in gossip, we feel guilty, uneasy, and ashamed. We also know the fear of being gossiped about when our own backs are turned, because those who gossip will betray their friends.

Our search for real growth in sobriety should include a willingness to part company with gossip. We also should not permit ourselves to gossip indirectly; that is, by pretending to "understand" another person to induce them to share personal information, or by introducing a subject with the intention of having gossip shared with us. We can also help ourselves by turning away from gossipy news stories and magazines. We cannot grow mentally and spiritually by reading about the misbehavior and shortcomings of others.

Knowing that my true good is in keeping straight, I will go through this one day without engaging in gossip.

JANUARY 6

NO NEED TO BE PERFECT

Perfectionism We recovering alcoholics often declare that we suffered from perfectionism while we were drinking. This did not mean that we did things perfectly or always met high standards. More than likely, it meant that we had grandiose ideas of the perfect people we wanted to be, but felt deep inadequacy about our failure to meet these high standards.

While we should develop good standards and values for our lives, we place an impossible demand on ourselves by wanting to be perfect in every way. What is this but a secret desire to be better than others, to occupy a superior position that will enable us to look down on others and, at the same time, to receive their approval and admiration?

In some manufacturing fields, there is a useful saying that serves as a guideline for inspectors: "Good enough is best." If something is good enough for its intended purpose, it may be equal to the best. If my performance and actions this day are good enough, it may be that they are as good as they have to be or as God wants them to be.

I will not expect impossible things from myself today. I will meet reasonable standards without permitting myself to become tense or strained.

JANUARY 7

ERASING OLD TAPES

Living Today   The human brain works like a tape recorder. With great fidelity, this built-in recorder stores up old memories that are recalled at surprising times. There are two kinds of these "old tapes" that are dangerous to the recovering alcoholic.

One dangerous old tape is a bitter memory of an unkind word or cruel action that hurt us deeply. This kind of memory comes back to destroy our peace of mind or to intensify feelings of low self-esteem.

Equally dangerous is another old tape: the recollection of a drinking experience that may have seemed enjoyable. When we run an old tape of this kind, we are revealing that we still wish we could drink.

Our recovery program shows us how to erase these old tapes. Bitter memories and resentments can be erased by forgiving the people who hurt us. We can eliminate the desire to relive pleasure in drinking experiences by looking honestly at the *total* effect of alcohol on our lives. We cannot relive the past, but we can use the lessons of the past to make our lives what they can be today.

Today, I will not be troubled by anything from the past. I cannot change what happened five minutes ago, but I can refuse to entertain thoughts that will harm me.

JANUARY 8

FINDING NEW VALUES

Restoration Recovering alcoholics sometimes waste time and energy brooding over lost opportunities, and we do have a record of many lost opportunities! Bill W., the cofounder of Alcoholics Anonymous, once made it big on Wall Street before crashing in the 1929 cataclysm. He later drank away two wonderful chances for a comeback. Most of us alcoholics can recall similar opportunities we lost by drinking. We can eliminate these regrets by practicing gratitude for the recovery we have made. Without rationalizing, we can remind ourselves that few opportunities would have benefited us if we had continued to drink.

We can take comfort, too, in the clear evidence that there's a wonderful restoration going on in our lives. While not every recovering alcoholic gets back a lost job or rebuilds a business, many of us do find sufficient prosperity and productive work in our new lives. Some alcoholics even find satisfying second careers or businesses after getting sober. Best of all, most recovering people discover that sobriety gives them the ability to appreciate their opportunities without worshipping material success.

I will make the best of my opportunities today and see them as stepping stones toward a more abundant life. I will not regret the past, because it brought necessary lessons.

COMING TO GRIPS WITH FEAR

Finding Courage Fear, a universal human emotion, strikes each of us in different ways. The brave parachute jumper may be afraid of public speaking, and the brilliant orator may have a fear of flying. An alcoholic's drinking is partly an attempt to cope with the feelings of fear. The recovering person, now having no drug, must face fear by using the tools of the program. The sober way to deal with fear is to *admit* that one has fears, to discuss them with a sponsor or another understanding person, and to seek the help of one's Higher Power in living with fear or having it removed.

When we share our experience with fear, we hear different kinds of stories. One person may declare that fear was completely removed by prayer. Another person, who prayed with what seemed to be the same degree of sincerity, may still be troubled by occasional fears. We cannot know exactly *how* the program will help each person cope with fear, but we can be confident that it will work for all of us. We have met fear successfully when we continue to stay sober and meet our responsibilities in all sorts of threatening situations.

I will not let fear keep me from any good thing today. My Higher Power can see me through any difficult or threatening situation.

NO NEED FOR ENVY

Overcoming Envy We alcoholics would be unusual people if we did not suffer from the common feeling of envy. Quite often, we are envious of people who surpass us in some activity or who threaten our self-esteem in some way. Even if we are high achievers in spite of our drinking, we might envy people who appear to be rivaling or overtaking us.

As recovering people, we can make choices about envy. We do not have to be envious of anybody when we fully accept ourselves and God's will for us. There is no reason to be envious of another if we are doing what God wants us to do and if we have turned our will and lives over to God.

We should be on guard for jealous feelings toward those close to us. Most of us can shrug when we read about strangers winning the million-dollar lottery, but how would we feel if a close friend or relative won? When those envious feelings surface, we might face them by admitting them to others and asking God's help in rising above them. And if we share these feelings in group discussions, others will be helped by our display of honesty.

I will accept myself as I am this day. I will not be jealous of anyone's status, possessions, or opportunities.

BEING DOWN

Overcoming Depression It would be difficult to find a group of people more subject to mood swings than alcoholics. While we were drinking, most of us were not perceptive enough to realize that our moods rose and fell in a rhythmic pattern. We did not mind being "up," but it distressed us greatly when we were "down." Alcohol was the "upper" most of us took when we were depressed.

In sobriety, there is usually no chemical "upper" that's safe to take for any of our down moods. Some of us have been helped by vitamins or by inspirational reading. But most of us simply have to ride out our down moods, doing the best we can until things are on the upswing again. In spite of being down, we do not have to drink.

Whatever the causes of mood swings, we can live with them, and we do not need any mood-altering drugs to see us through a down period. Our depression will pass, and we might even notice its hold lessening as we continue to grow in sobriety.

I will accept my feelings today, and I will not be disturbed if my mood seems somewhat low. This, too, will pass away.

JANUARY 12

IF IT FEELS GOOD . . .

Facing Other Excesses   In the drinking life, one of the flippant sayings we heard was, "If it feels good, do it!" We hear that less often in sobriety, although it sometimes appears on a bumper sticker or as a casual comment. And if we've learned anything in sobriety, we know that this remark is really a permit for disaster. We drank to feel good, but we often ended up feeling terrible.

Yet the same slogan, properly understood, can be useful for the recovering alcoholic. We all want to feel good. But a drink means temporary pleasure followed by pain, guilt, remorse, and ruin. This is not really feeling good. It is a nightmare of the worst feelings we can imagine.

Happy sobriety does feel good, even though it may include short-term discomfort or temporary boredom. The long-run tendency of sobriety is toward having peace of mind, feeling good about ourselves, and using our talents and opportunities wisely. This is the mature way to feel good, but we achieve it only by thinking and acting in the right ways. Perhaps our slogan could be, "If it will make you feel good now *and* in the future, do it!"

Today I will pass up anything that seems pleasurable in the short run but will make me guilty and unhappy later on.

JANUARY 13

THE NEED FOR APPROVAL

Raising Self-Esteem   Although drinking behavior may have been defiant and antisocial, most of us wanted others to think well of us. If we are not watchful, this need for approval can tyrannize us in sobriety.

A fierce need for approval can drive us to do more than our share of talking at discussion meetings. On the other hand, the fear of disapproval may cause us to "pass" when we really do have something to say. Outside of the fellowship, a strong desire for others' approval can make us anxious and unsure of ourselves. In the same way, a strong fear of being rejected or criticized can make us afraid to act.

In sobriety, we can free ourselves from an unreasonable desire for approval. When we learn to like ourselves more, we do not need constant reassurance and applause from others. We may also discover that we have been doing certain things against our will simply because we wanted somebody's approval. This is our fault, not theirs, and we can get such practices out of our lives when we no longer need them.

I will accept myself as I am today. I will give others the approval that I desire for myself. I will not try to win approval by being a people-pleaser.

IF GOD BE FOR US

Good Orderly Direction Sometimes recovering alcoholics find help and power in staying sober, yet feel naked and alone when facing other problems. It is almost as if they see their Higher Power as a "sobering-up God" who has said, "I'll help you with the drinking problem, but you're on your own in everything else."

The true way to practice AA's principles in all of our affairs is to view everything as spiritual, as being under God's direction and influence. God is with us in our homes, in the shop, on the highway, or wherever we go. There is no place and no action that is beyond God's scrutiny and power.

We should reflect on this truth at times when we are frustrated or when others threaten us. We should not expect God to aid us in manipulating or dominating others. God will be with us as a protecting, guiding presence in all our activities and relationships. And when we truly understand this, we will find surprising reserves of courage in situations that used to frighten us. This is true even when we are not certain of the outcome of a situation.

I will know that God is with me in all of my affairs today—in all that I think, say, or do.

JANUARY 15

NEVER TOO LATE

Self-Expression   In sobriety, many of us lament the fact that we wasted youthful years when we should have been earning college degrees or perfecting a skill. Many of us simply do not feel we can take up something new because we missed the opportunity to try it when we were younger.

We are now learning that age is mental, not really physical. Some people seem aged and beaten at twenty-five, while others act sprightly and young at sixty. Moreover, we can find wonderful examples of people who blossom out in new activities without any thought or concern about age barriers. It is never too late for a person to study, to take up a new trade or profession, to follow a new scientific or artistic interest, or to begin tennis or dance lessons.

If we are using age as a reason for not following our heart's desire, we should ask if we are really finding ways to avoid responsibility for our own performance in life. We may be seeking excuses to spare ourselves the struggle and effort that are always required when we do something new or challenging.

It is never too late to be the people God intended us to be.

I will give some thought today to the excuses I've been using for not making better use of my talents and opportunities.

MATERIAL THINGS MATTER

The Money Problem Now and then we have heated discussions about the role of material things in sobriety. Someone is bound to say that money can't buy happiness and that the spiritual has to come first.

But material things do matter in our lives, and we recovering alcoholics share with others the same desire to get ahead in life. We usually like good clothes, new automobiles, and steady paychecks. It is somewhat hypocritical to say that money and material things don't matter when we obviously need money and would like to have more of it.

Our problem with money and material things occurred when we made a god of them, when we saw worldly success as the end-all and be-all of life. The proper function of money is to provide for smooth exchange of the goods and services we must use in order to live. Far from denouncing money and material things, we can view them as spiritual gifts that should be used properly, but not worshipped. More than likely, we can appreciate material things in sobriety far more than we did in drinking, despite the exaggerated love we had then for worldly things.

I will neither despise material things nor make a god of them today. I will view them as part of God's plan, as things to use.

AVOIDING AA CHAUVINISM

Friendliness toward Others The term *chauvinism* has often been applied to men who are prejudiced toward women. But *chauvinism* has broader meanings as well. It is a belief in the alleged superiority of one's own nation or group. AA members can develop this peculiar chauvinism in supposing that there is some superiority in having survived alcoholism.

In the past, some of us have been particularly critical of non-alcoholics who choose to work in the alcoholism field. We may have relied on the axiom "It takes an alcoholic to understand an alcoholic" when in fact there are many people who have suffered from other problems and can understand our sufferings.

Perhaps one of the worst things about AA chauvinism is that it can offend people who could benefit from our principles and could become our allies in the work of helping alcoholics. While we have been highly successful in helping alcoholics, we still have not reached more than a small percentage of those who suffer. Additional breakthroughs are needed in the field of alcoholism, and the vital information might come from a nonalcoholic who empathizes with our suffering and wants to do something about it. Even AA has received some of its best ideas from nonalcoholics.

I will know today that membership in AA really means that I've found a rightful place in a larger fellowship: the human race. I'll view the world as a friendly place.

THE GREATEST THING IN THE WORLD

Love and Goodwill   In a famous sermon, Henry Drummond described love as a spectrum with nine ingredients. Love is patience, kindness, and generosity; it is humility, courtesy, and unselfishness. Finally, it is also good temper, guilelessness, and sincerity. Drummond called love the "greatest thing in the world."

Growth in sobriety includes improvement in all the nine ingredients that make up love. It has been fashionable in recent years to talk and sing about love as something the world needs, and we have an opportunity to practice love when we strengthen the qualities that make us loving people. And if we are uncomfortable with *love* as a word, we can call it *goodwill.*

If we are practicing the elements of love or goodwill, we won't have to sing about it or tell people what we're doing. They will see the change in our own lives and will be attracted by it. Love acts the part, and even people who cannot define love will respond to it. If love is present in our AA activities, it will cover a multitude of sins and will make up for many other shortcomings.

I'll try to practice the nine ingredients that make up love. Around difficult people, I'll remember that God's love is always present with us.

WILLPOWER ISN'T THE POWER

Power   AA members almost universally agree that willpower simply does not work as a direct force in overcoming alcoholism. The alcoholic who believes that a strong will and determination bring sobriety is probably headed for disaster.

In the same way, willpower is ineffective in dealing with a number of personal problems. In fact, the mustering of willpower seems to strengthen the problems or cause them to take other forms. We know that we are using willpower on problems when there is a great deal of tension and anxiety in our efforts. We are *fighting problems* rather than letting our Higher Power handle matters in a way that brings contentment and satisfaction. When excessive will is involved, we usually suppress feelings that ought to be expressed in positive ways.

The solution is not to fight problems in ourselves or in the outer world. By turning all matters over to the Higher Will, we will find the best way to deal with the evils within ourselves and with the opposition in our world. "Self-will run riot" was a problem in drinking, and it can be equally destructive in sobriety. Our will should be joined with the Higher Will for true success in living.

I will rely on my Higher Power as I go through the day. God can do for me the many things I cannot do for myself.

JANUARY 20

FIRST THINGS FIRST

Order   Busy people often declare, with some exasperation, that they cannot do everything at once. People with emotional problems, a group that includes many alcoholics, often feel that they are trying to do everything at once. Quite often, this pressure means that we waste our time fretting about all the things facing us, becoming totally ineffective as a result.

The simple slogan "First things first" shows us how to set priorities in an orderly way. In every situation or problem, there is always one step we can take that is more important than the others. Following that, we find a step of second importance, another of third importance, and so on. Sometimes, a certain action comes first simply because other things depend on it.

By using "First things first" as a guiding principle in our lives, we can live in an orderly, disciplined manner. If we have work to do today, we can plan to do the most important things first. If we have to reduce our activities, we can decide which activities we ought to retain. Having made these decisions, we can be at peace about our choices. We cannot do everything at once and we need not feel guilty about it.

Knowing that order is Heaven's first law, I'll do things today in an orderly manner.

GIVING WISELY IS SAFE

Helping Others   Most of us recovering alcoholics admit that we were selfish people when we drank. Even when we bought drinks for others, we did so either to seek their approval or in the expectancy that they would return the favor.

Our need in sobriety is to become unselfish by giving freely and cheerfully of ourselves. This, too, has it pitfalls. Feeling guilty about past selfishness, we may go overboard in helping others do things that they need to do for themselves. This can only lead to failure and disillusionment. It is common to hear AA members complain about people who are not in recovery despite help extended to them in finding a job, a place to live, and other necessities.

But in giving, it is not always right to look for a *quid pro quo*—something in return—or even for the other person's recovery and well-being. It's best to let the giving itself be its own reward. If we feel good about what we have done, we probably are doing the right things. Later on, when additional and unexpected rewards come to us, we can accept them as bonuses.

I can make progress in overcoming selfishness and self-centeredness if I give selflessly to others and take an honest interest in their problems.

NO HUMILIATION IN HUMILITY

Self-Understanding With few exceptions, every alcoholic eventually meets humiliation and defeat. This is especially painful in a world that places high value on winning and on having the approval and admiration of others. We feel diminished by these defeats. Nobody likes to be humbled, to be made to appear less than other people.

Yet these humiliations serve a constructive purpose if they lead us to seek humility. Truly humble people cannot really be humiliated, because they no longer rely on the false supports of worldly praise and approval. We develop humility as we withdraw from a reliance on our own powers and personality and realize that we ourselves can do nothing; it is our Higher Power who does the work.

Still, there is a paradox in humility. The person who admits he or she can do nothing will, in the process, tap into powers that were never available in the previous state of mind. In truth, humility is never humiliation or weakness, though these may lead to it. Humility is really a road to the power that only God can give us.

I'll watch myself today for the crazy things that set me up for humiliation. I won't try to impress others or win their admiration today. I will see humility as a most worthy condition.

JANUARY 23

THINKING WELL OF OURSELVES

Raising Self-Esteem Although there may have been conceit and cockiness in our past behavior, most of us suffered from feelings of low self-esteem. We alcoholics often felt alone and unworthy. Often, we had memories of parents and others who reminded us of our shortcomings or compared us unfavorably with others.

Whatever our past problems, we can raise our self-esteem in the present. We can begin by forgiving ourselves and others for past wrongs and mistakes. We must become willing to give up any belief or practice that causes us to dislike ourselves. We can remember that our self-esteem does not depend on achievements or on winning in competitions with others. Despite our failings, now and in the past, we are worthy in the sight of God and are entitled to God's grace.

Growth in the AA program usually brings growth in self-esteem. If we think well of ourselves, in the right sense, others will tend to think well of us, too. With proper self-esteem, we will not be crushed or dismayed when someone seems to dislike us. Our feelings about ourselves will be much more than a mirror of others' opinions.

I will think well of myself today. I will not put myself down, even jokingly. I will know that if God is for me, no one can be against me.

NO HIDDEN THOUGHTS

Moral Inventory   It is fortunate that we can think in secret, because our thoughts would quickly get us in trouble if others could read them. In our thoughts, we can choose what we wish to reveal to others before we speak or act.

In the long run, however, we do not really conceal our true thoughts and feelings. The nature of our thoughts shapes our character and becomes part of us. It even affects our appearance. It is not difficult at all to identify people who are fearful, angry, or jealous.

This process has its good side, because kind thoughts and feelings also affect our appearance, and in positive ways. Norman Vincent Peale wrote that "God runs a beauty parlor," meaning that plain people with gracious thoughts tend to become more attractive as years wear on.

As AA members, we need not fear our own thoughts and feelings if we are continuing to work the program. As the sober years stretch out, we will be improving our thoughts and feelings, and this will tell others what the program is doing for us and through us.

I'll remember today that I don't really keep my thoughts and feelings secret. I will think well of myself and all others. I know that there are no hidden thoughts in the long run.

FINDING A HIGHER GOOD

Handling Trouble   There are times when things just don't work out, despite our best efforts. Even in sobriety, we can have business or marriage failures, accidents, sicknesses, or trouble in holding a job. Sobriety is no guarantee that things will always work out according to our expectancies.

But no disappointment or failure has to throw us or cause permanent distress. It is some comfort to remember that the meeting of the first two AA members came out of a business failure, not a success. On many occasions, a disappointment or a setback can actually give a person the insight and understanding needed for a new, more successful effort.

We do not, of course, want to rationalize failure. We should also accept responsibility when failure has been the result of negligence or wrong action on our part. Nevertheless, as we continue to seek and to follow God's guidance, we will find the course of our lives that fits our needs and capabilities. There is a higher good in everything. Even our drinking was indirectly beneficial in pushing us toward AA and the program's healing principles.

I will not waste time today brooding over mistakes or losses. I'll know that God is in charge of my life and can turn liabilities into assets and defeats into victories.

JANUARY 26

PRAY FOR POTATOES

Faith and Works   One of the sayings heard at AA meetings is "Pray for potatoes *but* grab a hoe." This says that both prayer and action are needed to get favorable results in our lives.

But recovering alcoholics do not really need to be told to "grab a hoe." One of our problems is that we often worked too hard for certain ends, only to lose out in the long run. What we really need to know is that our prayers work *with* our actions to bring about good results. The saying should be "Pray for potatoes *and* grab a hoe." Faith and action are both needed.

In the strong belief that God is working through us, we can do our own work with confidence and gratitude. Our own efforts are strengthened when we know that we are not alone. We may even receive inspiration and new understanding as we continue on this path. Changes in our lives will turn out to be positive and beneficial if we remind ourselves that God is in charge of the process.

Under the right conditions, potatoes grow in a miraculous way. Other projects will also come to maturity in our lives under God's direction.

I will be grateful for the opportunity to work today. Moreover, I will know that a Higher Power is living and working in my life.

JANUARY 27

LIVE AND LET LIVE

Tolerance For countless reasons, people with drinking problems blunder into conflicts with others. It's not unusual to hear that a person has not spoken to a relative for years as a result of some foolish misunderstanding. Some of us, sad to say, cling to old grievances even after we come into AA.

The key to peace in our lives is the slogan "Live and let live." If we reflect on this slogan a bit, we realize that it's a form of the Golden Rule. We want to live freely, and we ought to let others choose their lifestyles without interference from us. After all, if there was anything we alcoholics resented, it was the busybody who tried to shape our lives for us.

Nobody has the competence or understanding to tell us how we should live, nor should we try to control other people. We have a big job to do in overcoming our own faults and solving our own problems. We have neither the time nor the wisdom to run other people's lives.

"Live and let live," if followed by every person and nation, would bring universal peace. We can use the slogan wisely to end conflicts in our lives and to terminate new ones before they develop into serious problems.

I'll remember today that nobody appointed me guardian of my neighbors' manners and morals. I have a full-time job keeping myself straight.

JANUARY 28

EASY DOES IT

Avoiding Tension   As people of excess, alcoholics tend to swing between periods of great activity and times of complete lassitude. There is a tendency to waste time at one point, and then to overcompensate for it by working feverishly and frantically to catch up. Both ways are out of balance.

We need to approach life in a relaxed manner, letting the natural rhythm of events take over and do some of the work for us. Too much effort defeats itself. The overanxious person strives too hard and makes things worse, like the salesman who talks too long and kills the sale.

In the AA way of life, we expect and accept responsibilities. But we are not slavishly committed to success at any price. We make a full commitment to any project we undertake, and we do our best at all times. Then we let things unfold rather than trying to force them.

It is also common to hear people say, "Easy does it, but do it!" This is a reminder that the slogan is not a prescription for laziness and indifference. It is also a reminder to avoid high-pressure tactics and excessive pushing.

I'll let things work out today. I'll do what has to be done, without feeling that the world will collapse without me.

WILLINGNESS IS THE KEY

Strong Desire Although willpower alone does not work in overcoming alcoholism, there is a place for the will, or willingness, in the search for happy sobriety. Things can happen if we are willing to let them happen. More important, progress often depends on our willingness to give up what stands in our way. It also requires our willingness to take the actions necessary for success.

This same willingness, so vital to finding sobriety, is also applicable in other areas of our lives. The pioneers of AA suggested that getting sober required being willing to go to any lengths. This is the key to other achievements and to the overcoming of problems besides alcohol.

We often have to put up with unpleasant conditions simply because we do not want to change them badly enough. For example, we may dislike the unpleasant coughing and risks of smoking, but lack the willingness to quit. We may brood over lost opportunities, but be unwilling to take advantage of the opportunities we have now.

The key to constructive change in our lives is willingness—and that applies to other matters as well as to alcohol.

I'll try to be honest today about what I really want. I will remind myself that if I want something badly enough, willingness is the key to action and to success.

NO JUSTIFIED RESENTMENTS

Personal Inventory One of the greatest hurdles in sobriety is the so-called justified resentment. We feel that we have a right to be angry at somebody who has hurt or offended us. This feeling might be correct if our anger could remedy the matter and bring it to a just conclusion, but this hardly ever happens. If we are angry, we usually want revenge more than we want justice. Uncontrolled anger will make us behave as unjustly as those who harmed us did. This means more trouble.

Whether revenge is sought or not, anger also poisons our own lives. Emmet Fox compared it to the insane practice of drinking prussic acid. People cannot take a drink of acid and then assign it to the person they detest. They will bear its effects in their own bodies. In the same way, our anger produces its own acids, which destroy our peace of mind and make us ineffective.

We can deal with "justified resentment" by reminding ourselves that there's no justification for the pain and sickness a festering resentment will cause in our lives. There is no justified "first drink," and in the same way, there is no justified resentment.

Today I may have to swim against the tide by not getting upset over matters that enrage others. I will not let myself be drawn into the angry currents around me.

OPEN-MINDEDNESS MEANS GROWTH

Facing Change While open-mindedness is supposedly virtuous, many of us have difficulty with it. In our drinking, we continued to suffer because we were unwilling to believe that anything could relieve us of our condition. We also feared that change would diminish us.

Our great liberation came in opening up our minds to new ideas. This same process might be needed in sober living. We may have an investment in old attitudes and ideas that are keeping us from constructive growth. Without giving up our attitudes immediately, we can at least give new ideas honest consideration and study.

True open-mindedness does not mean empty-mindedness. We still can have strong convictions, consistent values, and definite opinions. But in the spirit of open-mindedness, we should continuously reexamine our views and adopt new ideas for improvement and growth.

Open-mindedness helped bring us to sobriety. It can also open the doors to other blessings that will bring enrichment and happiness.

I will be open-minded and curious today. New ideas can bring wonderful benefits to me if I am willing to consider them.

February

FEBRUARY 1

GARBAGE IN, GARBAGE OUT

Releasing the Past One thing we don't need in our lives is garbage from the past. Yet many alcoholics say that old thoughts and bitter memories often sneak devilishly back to spoil what should have been a pleasant day. Why do we let garbage from the past befoul our lives a second time?

Computer programmers use a certain expression when their systems turn up errors: "Garbage In, Garbage Out." If you feed erroneous, useless information into a computer, that's what you get back.

We seem to have built-in computers that work the same way. If we waste time and energy talking about past injustices or old mistakes, we are unwittingly calling them back into our lives. We are bringing back garbage that should have been discarded permanently to make room for better things.

There is no benefit in bringing back old garbage. We can't change the past. We can't change our mistakes by brooding about them, and we can't obtain justice by remembering how badly we were treated or by plotting revenge. When we bring back garbage, we allow it to occupy space that should be devoted to constructive and positive things.

If we don't want garbage in our lives, let's not put it there by bringing up matters that should have been released, forgiven, and forgotten.

I will keep my mind on the present, knowing that a positive attitude will help me make the best of the opportunities that come to me.

WHY DO YOU NEED THOSE MEETINGS?

Staying Active Friends and relatives are often grateful when they witness an alcoholic's dramatic recovery after years of horror and pain. However, they sometimes fail to understand the importance of meetings after the alcoholic has been sober for months or years. "Do you have to go to *another* meeting this week?" a spouse might say. "Aren't you overdoing it a bit?" Or a friend might say, "You're sober now. Why do you need *those* people?"

Some AA members probably do use the meetings simply as a social outlet and attend more than they need. But no other person can really determine what you or I need to maintain sobriety. Moreover, even in sobriety, we are always dealing with alcohol, which can come back into our lives with stunning force if we ever become careless or foolish. It is much better to go to *more* meetings than we need than to attend too few or none at all.

There is another side as well. The meetings need *us*. By attending meetings, we are carrying the AA message and providing a haven for desperate newcomers who need our help.

However, we should be tolerant and understanding when others are critical of our zealous attendance of meetings. It is not necessary that they understand our need. It is only necessary that we understand!

I will remember today that the price of liberty is eternal vigilance. I don't want to change anything—including meeting attendance—that is necessary for my continued sobriety.

FEBRUARY 3

NO COINCIDENCES

Guidance The early history of AA still sparkles with fortunate coincidences that moved the fellowship forward. It was miraculous, for example, that Bill W.'s telephone call in 1935 was to a woman who "just happened" to know Dr. Bob, a suffering alcoholic.

When we are in tune with AA's spiritual program, we know with absolute certainty that there really are no chance events or coincidences. Our Higher Power is in charge and all things really are working together for good, even though this is not always apparent at first.

If we let this Higher Power guide and direct our lives, we will be thrilled and delighted by a number of wonderful coincidences. We may happen to pick up the magazine or book that gives us information we need. We might take the wrong bus or subway and meet a person whose advice changes our lives. Or we follow a hunch and make an unusual decision that leads to a number of opportunities we never dreamed of.

We cannot force these fortunate "coincidences" to happen or direct their course, except by following the program every day. But we never need fret about the future if we have placed our lives in God's hands. There are no coincidences—only the hand of God ceaselessly at work.

I will work this day as if everything depended on me, but at the same time I will know that everything really depends on God.

FEBRUARY 4

THE REWARDS OF HONESTY

Honesty Sometimes we think that honesty is simply too painful and demanding—all sacrifice with no gain. If we are completely honest with ourselves, however, the results can only be positive.

What are the advantages of being entirely honest about our motives and feelings? One benefit is that we never will have to face the disillusionment and humiliation that come from self-deception. Surely we had enough of that while drinking.

Honesty also speaks for itself. People know intuitively when a person is completely honest, and they are drawn to that person because of it. An honest AA member—one who has truly faced personal faults—also becomes an example to others.

The honest person has self-respect and a clear conscience. In real honesty, there is no inner struggle to keep up appearances or to pretend we are anybody except ourselves.

Honesty makes us comfortable rather than pained, relaxed rather than anxious, and decisive rather than confused. These are rich rewards for people who once lived in the false world of alcoholism.

I'll try to be honest in all things today. In any case, I will at least be honest with myself about my true motives and feelings.

FEBRUARY 5

IS IT REALLY HONESTY?

Honesty No matter how cruel the results, the need to criticize others can be a compulsion. Such criticism is sometimes justified by the defense "Well, I had to be honest" or "It was only the truth."

But is it really honesty to gratuitously bring out a hurtful truth? Not when the critic's real motives are to wound and humiliate someone, not to foster self-improvement and better behavior. Under those circumstances, the critic is really the dishonest person—for not having detected the ugly personal motives that triggered the criticism.

Honesty is closely related to humility, and the truly honest person is usually humbly aware of personal shortcomings in his or her own life. This alone makes the honest person reluctant to criticize and always careful to do it in ways that avoid inflicting pain or hurt.

Real honesty is rare, especially in people who hurt others under the guise of honesty.

With God's help, I'll look carefully at my motives today. It's possible that I could be using honesty as an excuse for putting others down.

FEBRUARY 6

COMPETING WITH OTHERS

A New View of Competition   We live in a world torn by endless strife and competition. Although competitiveness can be a good quality, we've seen it become very ugly and destructive. A few alcoholics like the excitement of competition, but many of us withdraw from it. We hate anything that includes the risk of defeat or might make us appear second-best. Sometimes we even feel guilty in winning!

We don't need the kind of competition that causes us to gloat arrogantly in victory or to wallow in self-pity in defeat. We don't really need to compete with others in anything if we are truly seeking guidance from our Higher Power. If God is in charge of our lives, we do not have to struggle with others for the good we seek in life. It is God's pleasure to give us the good things of the kingdom.

There is a kind of competition that does pay off in sobriety—competition with ourselves. We can try to be better people than we might have been yesterday, or a week ago, or a month ago. This kind of competition requires skill and stamina, and it also requires exercise and training. But anybody who sincerely seeks a spiritual life and true self-improvement can find it in AA.

This day, I won't try to reform or change anybody but myself. I'll remember that God is in charge of things and concentrate on competing with the person I once was by letting the program work in my life.

FEBRUARY 7

RESPONSIBILITY FOR OUR ACTIONS

Maturity The practice of scapegoating goes way back to biblical times. It's easier to blame others for our problems than to take personal responsibility for facing and solving these problems.

In the AA program, however, there's nothing that serves as a basis for blaming others. In every way, AA insists that alcoholics take personal responsibility—not only for finding and maintaining sobriety, but also for past wrongs and personal shortcomings. This is a difficult change for alcoholics who have believed that many of their problems were caused by others.

But being forced to take responsibility for our actions is a blessing in disguise. It fairly shouts the good news that we can take charge of our lives despite what others think and do. With God's help, we can change ourselves into the people we ought to be. We are fortunate that life is arranged to give us this personal responsibility— where would we be if our recovery depended only on others?

We also learn that this responsibility is not limited to our drinking. We are responsible for everything we think and do, and we have the power to make improvements in our lives beginning today.

I will go through the day without blaming others for my problems. I will feel grateful today that I am responsible, that personal responsibility is part of my God-given free will.

RIGHT ATTITUDES TOWARD ANONYMITY

Traditions At both the practical and spiritual levels, anonymity is a great blessing for the AA fellowship. There is much wisdom behind Traditions Eleven and Twelve.

Yet, it is possible to use anonymity as a cloak for pride and fear. This might be the case with alcoholics who insist on concealing their AA membership from fellow workers, neighbors, and friends. They defend this zealous protection of their anonymity by pointing to the traditions. However, this could reveal a lack of understanding and perhaps a lack of commitment to the program.

Why is it useful to let others know we belong to AA? Our best opportunities to help others may come from people who watched us in sobriety and were inspired by our example.

However, we must maintain anonymity at the public media level, and nobody has a right to violate another person's anonymity. Nor is it wise to be critical of the AA member who prefers anonymity at every level. We have no right to pass judgment on such decisions. Above all, we never have a right to break another's anonymity.

I'll try to set a good example for others who may be seeking sobriety. I can find guidance about anonymity.

GETTING STARTED TODAY

Responsible Activity For the recovering person, every assignment or day's work can have a disagreeable moment. The problem is getting started—overcoming our fear of taking the plunge.

The real problem is deeper than the wish to avoid mere unpleasantness. Some of our resistance to getting started may be fear of failure. It could also be a deep-seated desire to live in a problem-free environment, where all of our needs can be met without effort on our part. It can even be a desire to return to the quest for constant excitement and stimulation.

We need to know that our answer is in *guidance* and *acceptance.* If we have truly committed our will and lives to the care and keeping of our Higher Power, we will find the right path for each day's work. We can also accept any work or challenge that occurs, knowing it is part of a higher order for our lives. Our current situation may be depressing or boring, but it can easily be a stepping stone to our long-term good.

I will meet today's challenges and responsibilities with gratitude and confidence, knowing that God is guiding and directing my life.

WHAT IS RIGHTFULLY MINE

Personal Gains   One of the hard lessons of life is that we can't always "win" in the worldly game for prestige, power, and property. It is especially galling to see rewards going to others who don't seem to have earned them. Much of the world's conflict, in fact, grows out of disputes over what rightfully belongs to whom.

In sobriety, we need a higher perspective than what we're likely to find in the brawling world around us. Rather than demanding rights to anything, we should know that everything is part of a spiritual world. The real meaning of the last line of The Lord's Prayer is that all power, prestige, and property belong to our Higher Power. Whatever we have or will acquire is only temporary, at best, and can easily be lost through wrong thinking and bad actions.

Emmet Fox, whose writings guided the early AA members, taught that we possess things only through "rights of consciousness." In perfectly legitimate ways, we will always possess whatever is necessary for our real work in this life. If one door closes, another will always open. We do not have to envy anything that others possess, nor should we attempt to wrestle it from them. God will always lead us to whatever we need for our highest good.

I will not fret this day about any lost property or opportunities. My needs will be met in a satisfactory manner as I continue to seek the highest and best in every situation.

PRACTICE MAKES PATIENCE

Acquiring Maturity Extreme impatience is part of most alcoholic stories: "I want what I want when I want it." When it continues in sobriety, impatience leads to mistakes and accidents. How can we bring impatience under control without losing all drive and initiative?

One route may be to acquire patience through *practice.* We can devote some time each day to a task that must be done, even if it is tedious and boring. We can make a real effort to be more patient with somebody who is slow or difficult. We can face the fear and anxiety that sometimes make us overwork or turn us into people-pleasers.

These exercises won't eliminate impatience overnight. But they'll produce the satisfaction of knowing that we're getting control of our lives. They will also make us more effective in our dealings with others.

Reminding ourselves that all outcomes are in God's hands can help us acquire patience. Willful pushing does not bring the serenity and well-being we really seek. We labor in vain if we are seeking goals that are not in line with God's will for us.

I'll do my work today with the knowledge that God really is in charge of my life—I do not have to let anything or anyone rob me of my serenity and self-control. I will practice patience in situations where it is needed.

DO IT SOBER

Practicing Principles There may be a hidden meaning in that bumper sticker that reminds us to "Do it sober," but we can also read it to mean that *real* sobriety should guide *everything* we do today.

Real sobriety is emotional sobriety. We have it when our principles protect us from overpowering feelings growing out of greed, fear, and resentment. Even without the bottle, an attack of fear or resentment can distort personal judgment and lead to foolish mistakes. Whatever we do, whether it's sweeping a factory floor or leading a corporate board meeting, we should do with confidence and calm self-control.

When we work in this way, we help others. We only harm them if we bring bitterness and resentment into their space. True emotional sobriety helps us set a better example and assures others that AA really works in people's lives. One AA member was pleasantly surprised when he was complimented for remaining calm in confrontations with angry people. He realized that his AA principles had been at work in his workplace, helping him to maintain a calm dignity that made him assertive and effective. Whatever we do sober, we always do better.

Today I'll remind myself to stay emotionally as well as physically sober. So-called dry drunks are not slips, but they destroy my effectiveness and should have no place in my life. I will meet everyone and face everything with quietness and confidence.

WHEN OTHERS DON'T PERFORM

Personal Responsibility There will be times when other people will disappoint us—either intentionally or because of indifference or incompetence. If we have been counting on them, their nonperformance can cause us real anger and frustration.

Our growth, however, should teach us that such failures are part of life. While never losing trust in others, we must accept them as fallible people. Their mistakes and lapses come from the human shortcomings all of us have.

Our best course is to live without expecting too much from others. They are not here to please or satisfy us. It's possible, too, that we've been unrealistic in some of our expectations and have set ourselves up for disappointments.

Our personal responsibility is to do our best even when others fall short of our expectations. At the same time, we can grow by becoming more reliable and dependable ourselves.

We cannot use another's failure as an excuse for negligence on our part.

Today I'll expect the best, but I will know that I also have the spiritual resources to deal with the worst that can happen.

FEBRUARY 14

RELEASING THE PAST

Living in the Present Some of us waste time brooding over past failures and lost opportunities. Since the past is beyond our reach, we can't change anything that happened. We do, however, have the power to change the way we view the present. We can begin by realizing that our past troubles really may have been valuable lessons.

We can also get a better perspective by releasing the idea that anything from the past controls our future. The real meaning of the saying "With God, all things are possible" is that our Higher Power can transform anything that happened in our past. AA has had its share of miraculous changes that came to people who seemingly had lost all hope. These changes have included miraculous restorations in health, finances, and relationships.

A new saying is that something or some person who bothered us in the past is history, as far as we're concerned. Let's put history where it belongs—on the shelves and away from our daily thinking and activities.

I can be a new person today and every day. The past cannot control or limit me, but I do benefit from its lessons.

FEBRUARY 15

AA IS AN AUTOMATIC SPRINKLER SYSTEM

Emotional Emergencies Wise managers install automatic sprinkler systems to protect their businesses. The system's great value is that it goes into action during the first few minutes of a fire, before it gets out of control. This gives the fire department precious time to arrive and put the fire out.

Our AA program gives us something like an automatic sprinkler system. We never know when the flames of resentment might leap up, seemingly out of nowhere. If we've been working our program, something takes over automatically to begin dealing with resentment.

This gives us time to bring more of our valuable spiritual tools into use. Knowing that resentment is burning away, we can try one thing and then another until it is brought to rest. Perhaps we will try prayer. We might also discuss our problem with a close friend or sponsor. Maybe we'll attend a meeting and lay the matter out for group attention. We may help somebody, even in a small way. An amazing healing of resentment can come from any helpful action. Even a simple action like helping a person in a stalled automobile can work wonders in deflecting the pain of ongoing resentment.

I need not fear the sudden appearance of resentment if I have been following my program. I already have within myself the methods for holding resentment at bay while I deal with it.

FEBRUARY 16

MENTAL ARGUMENTS ARE BAD THINKING

Serenity Again and again we hear that bad thinking and drinking are linked together. Bad thinking is any line of thought that tends to be destructive. Mental arguments are in that class because they destroy peace of mind and self-control. We can avoid them by learning acceptance and maintaining serenity at all costs.

Sometimes we engage in mental arguments with those who seem to have defeated us or put us down. This only gives more life to the hurt we have been feeling; in effect, we cooperate in hurting ourselves repeatedly. Even the satisfaction of letting ourselves "win" the mental argument doesn't really settle the matter.

We can maintain our serenity in all situations by accepting people as they are. We are not responsible for changing their opinions. We must also accept and dismiss past mistakes and failures, no matter who was at fault. We owe it to ourselves not to destroy another moment's happiness with futile mental arguments that serve no good purpose in our lives.

Once we dismiss mental arguments, we can give our time and attention to things that really matter.

I will not waste a single second on any kind of mental argument. Anything another person said or did is forgiven and forgotten, and it has no power to hurt me a second time.

FEBRUARY 17

BE CAREFUL WHAT YOU PRAY FOR

Choosing the Right Goals "Be careful what you pray for," the Old-Timers said, for you are likely to get it. While this sounds exciting, it's really an important warning. Prayers are currents of thought directed toward a goal. The goal must be something we want to live with once it is achieved. What often happens, unfortunately, is that we seek things that turn out to be shallow and even harmful after we get them. Such disillusionment has been the stuff of countless morality tales.

Our bitter experience with alcohol can also furnish lessons about the kinds of goals we should strive for in sobriety. Let's take an inventory if we find ourselves thinking that our happiness depends on certain people, places, or things. Our true happiness comes from our Higher Power and the right combination of love and service. With the right attitude, we can actually be happy under many kinds of conditions and with all sorts of people.

What, then, should we pray for? "Knowledge of [God's] will for us and the power to carry that out" is a prayer that puts things in proper order. Seek to do God's will, and you might be utterly amazed at the results. After all, it is God's pleasure to give you good things.

I'll pray for knowledge of God's will today, while exercising prudence in all my affairs. I'll be willing to let myself be surprised by the interesting things that can happen.

SHINING SHOES FOR SUBORDINATES

Growing in Humility   Did you ever hear of a man named Samuel Logan Brengle? He was a Salvation Army officer whose spiritual consciousness was legendary. But he didn't start out that way. A gifted ministerial student of the nineteenth century, he joined the Salvation Army only to find himself sent to a cellar to clean the shoes of other cadets–most of them far below him in learning and intelligence.

Brengle used that humbling experience to conquer his pride and resentment. He later recalled the utter joy he felt as he cleaned the shoes and prayed for each person. Later on, Brengle became an inspiration to thousands.

It's not likely any of us will have to clean shoes for subordinates today. What's more likely is that we'll encounter situations that wound our pride or churn up resentment. We can turn any such experience into an opportunity for growth by praying to see God's hand in the matter and refusing to fight about it. The peace and serenity we feel is our reward, and, like Brengle, we'll become better people who can be of real service to others.

Somebody may come at me today with something that makes my blood boil. I won't be a doormat, but I will remember that I always have the choice of making anything a positive, spiritually uplifting experience.

STICKING WITH THE WINNERS

Prudence   "Stick with the winners," newcomers are told at Twelve Step meetings. The real message of this statement is to share the attitudes and actions of people who are successful in living sober.

No recovering person can have a successful day while dwelling on ideas that can be harmful. We'll meet people in the course of the day whose attitudes may appall us. We may work with people who are critical, gossipy, or resentful. It's not our duty to correct them or argue with them. We're wise, however, not to accept what we recognize as wrong thinking.

Winners, in AA terms, are people who seek sobriety first and live up to the principles of the program. Seek them out for help in doing likewise.

I'll try to associate with people who exemplify the highest and best in good attitudes. While I will not snub anyone, I'll look for closeness with people who want to grow in sobriety.

A DAY OF ACCEPTANCE

Releasing the Past "We will not regret the past nor fear the future," goes one of the promises in Twelve Step programs. Neither the past nor the future should control what we're thinking and doing today. After all, if our Higher Power is everything, no person or action can be outside of this supreme control.

Today, I will rise above anything that was said or done in the past. I will also hold the idea that the future is bright with promise, and that this promise will be fulfilled. Nobody's opinion or criticism can be unsettling to me if my beliefs and self-worth are anchored in my Higher Power.

It's true that there might have been lots of wreckage in the past—even more recently when we have been living sober. It doesn't matter. In amazing ways, our Higher Power sometimes turns negative conditions into future benefits. This was actually what happened when our compulsive condition led directly to a new way of life.

I will accept life today and will look for unexpected blessings. No person or group can keep me from good as I accept God's direction in my life.

"In all your ways acknowledge [God, who] shall direct your paths." I'll remember this frequently as I go about the day.

UNEXPECTED DISAPPOINTMENTS

Acceptance As life unfolds, we sometimes get unexpected disappointments that seem undeserved—the car breaks down, a business deal goes sour, or a close friend betrays us. As alcoholics, most of us don't handle such things too well. "Why me, Lord?" we often respond.

Our best approach is simply to view life as a mixture of bitter and sweet, knowing that we've been given real mastery over conditions. We cannot always be sure that a disappointment really is as bad as it seems to be, and sometimes it can become a step toward our good. As one alcoholic phrased it, "Some of the worst things that have happened turned out to be the best."

It's good to face the day with optimism, with confidence, and even with some excitement about the opportunities ahead. If we're maintaining sober thinking, everything that happens today will be transformed into gains for tomorrow—all our tomorrows. We're on a spiritual journey that goes far beyond anything we're doing here and now.

I won't expect to be disappointed today, but I'll know that nothing can really upset or disturb me without my permission.

STAYING ON COURSE

Power in Purpose   When riding in an airplane on automatic pilot, I marvel at the way the aircraft stays on course even while bouncing and shaking through pockets of turbulence. Even more significant is the pilot's calm indifference to these minor movements as he checks occasionally to make sure the plane continues on the right course.

Many things that happen to us each day are no more important than the routine turbulence an aircraft encounters. But as sick, compulsive people, we sometimes view every disturbance as a terrible storm and become panicky or enraged over things that are of little consequence in the long run. "I could accept a major calamity, but a broken fingernail ruined my day," one speaker said at an AA meeting.

We can set our lives on "automatic pilot" by choosing continuing recovery as our major goal and letting all things fall in line with that. The turbulence of ordinary living cannot deflect us from our true course if we calmly accept it as natural, unavoidable, and nonthreatening. Even if a real storm blows up and gives us anxious moments, we can stay on the recovery course we have chosen.

Disappointments and annoyances are part of the human condition. I will be cheerful and optimistic today even if I am bounced around a bit. There is within me an automatic pilot, through which my Higher Power leads me to continued recovery and true fulfillment as a person.

WE ALWAYS HAVE CHOICES

Decision Making   Self-pity is often rooted in the strong feeling that we have been victimized by people or conditions. "I never had a chance" and "You deceived me!" are common complaints that reveal self-pity.

It is astonishing and humbling to learn that we always have choices, even when other people or bad conditions are grinding us down. One of the great discoveries of the Twelve Step movement is that alcoholics could begin to recover no matter how helpless they had become, no matter how far they had slid into defeat and despair. Once a decision was made to seek sobriety as a primary goal, other choices and decisions became possible.

We choose our attitudes and responses. We have neither the power nor the right to control others, but we can choose to soften our attitudes toward them, and we can forgive and release people we don't like.

We can always choose how we want to think and feel. It may take effort to break the habit of feeling victimized and sorry for ourselves, but our Higher Power will show us the way if we decide that is what we really want.

Nobody can ruffle my feathers today or make me feel oppressed and victimized. I can always make choices that will enhance my sobriety and place me on a better footing for the days ahead.

FEBRUARY 24

SELFISHNESS

Self-Improvement We're told again and again
that we have to be selfish about our own recovery,
but this seems to be in conflict with the fact that
selfishness is the root of our problem. How can
selfishness be both good and bad?

The selfishness we need for recovery is a devo-
tion to self-improvement, rather than the selfish
indulgence that made us sick. One is a giving of
ourselves, the other is frantic taking that leads to
destruction. The person who seeks self-improvement is competing only against his or her former
self. The sick brand of selfishness, on the other
hand, is usually involved in unhealthy competition with others.

There is an easy way to test whether our selfishness is the right kind. If our conduct leads to
long-term happiness and higher self-esteem, it is
probably right. If it harms us or others, something
is wrong. We can correct this by getting back to
the basics of the program and pursuing self-
improvement rather than self-indulgence.

**Just for today, I will take part only in that which
will obviously benefit everyone. I will not put my
own concerns ahead of others'; but at the same
time, I will not let others take advantage of me.**

MALICIOUS GOSSIP

Honest Motives "Without really knowing what was happening, I said something bad today about a person I secretly resented. When it occurred to me that my remark could come back to hurt me, I had a moment of panic," an AA member said. "With a little reflection, however, I realized that the more serious problem was the dishonesty that caused me to belittle somebody behind his back!"

We are growing up when we come to see that gossip feeds on our own insecurity and self-deception. When we are unwilling to part company with gossip, we devise subtle ways to keep it in our lives. We can gossip by steering the conversation to a topic that is likely to bring revealing comments. We also gossip by reveling in lurid accounts of others' sins and failings. We should even ask ourselves if we are gossiping when we "discuss" another member who is not living up to our ideas of true Twelve Step standards. This is often prefaced by the remark, "I don't want to take Joe's inventory, but . . ."

We cannot live freely and happily if we practice gossip in any form. The practice may be hidden, but it leaves us with guilt, fear, and shame. We cannot gossip and be completely trustworthy and reliable.

I will truly mind my own business today. Forgiving myself for past excursions into gossip, I will say nothing about others behind their backs. If somebody has gossip to share, I will politely move to another topic.

THE FIX THAT NEVER WAS

Recovery In all of the despair and defeat that went along with drinking, most of us held to the ideal of a "fantastic fix"—a drinking experience so fulfilling and complete that it would solve our problems and leave us searching no more.

Compulsive disorders, like alcoholism, seem to include this delusion. The gambler looks for the big score, the overeater seeks the total enjoyment of food, and the sex junkie searches for the perfect partner. But the search never ends, because our compulsions always drive us to seek stronger wine and greater excitement.

The only fix that will ever work has to be rooted in sobriety and right living. When we think and live properly, free from alcohol, we find a fix that really works. We find continuous satisfaction instead of soaring excitement, sound relationships with other people instead of ego-gratifying encounters, and purpose instead of drifting.

The peak experience we had been seeking is a fix that never can be. We can be truly "fixed" only by staying sober.

I will live calmly and gratefully today, forgetting the drive for excitement that was destroying me. My Higher Power knows who I am and what I should be doing.

SELLING MYSELF

Personal Relations Thoughtful people tell us that every person has to "sell" himself or herself in daily work. As alcoholics, we can find that threatening. Uncertainty and the fear of rejection or failure put us under stress.

We can avoid this stress and tension by putting all responsibility for results in God's hands. While it is true that we want to succeed and to be accepted, we can never be sure that our idea of success is the right one. There are times when our strong determination to succeed at all costs makes us overbearing and demanding in our approach. We may be so anxious to appear competent and knowledgeable that we overreach ourselves and make stupid blunders.

God can show us how to handle each day's affairs in an orderly, reasonable way. It is not necessary to win every argument or to make every sale. We can sell ourselves more effectively when we go through the day calmly and take a genuine interest in the ideas and concerns of others.

I will look upon my customers and fellow workers as friends and allies. I do not have to bludgeon every person into accepting my point of view. If I am sincerely trying to follow God's will in all my affairs, others will sense my sincerity and will be glad to consider what I have to say.

SEEKING EXCITEMENT

Seeking Serenity "I haven't found anything to replace the excitement I felt while drinking," a member complained. "Sure, I'm grateful to be sober. But sometimes it's so darned boring!"

Let's talk about that need for excitement, or "high." For many of us, it was an important part of our drinking. At times, our drinking *was* exciting—it came with celebrations, graduations, marriage receptions, engagements, and just about anything else out of the ordinary. Along with it, we wanted other excitement: exciting love affairs, exciting experiences, exciting stories.

For us, however, excitement always ended with a crash, often a terrible one. Waking up after an exciting binge was a horrible moment. It stretched out to become more horrible. It never seemed to have a happy ending.

We can take this addiction to excitement in hand by recognizing it as a component of our alcoholism. We'll still be able to be excited at times, but it must be a type of excitement that brings neither crash nor hangover.

I will not let boredom push me into actions that I know will be destructive in the long run. I do not want thrills at the expense of my self-respect and sense of well-being.

FEBRUARY 29

MAKING AMENDS

Erasing Guilt Why do we feel guilty about so many things? It is true that we ought to feel remorse and regret about deliberate wrongs, but we did not cause most of the world's woes, and we are powerless to change many of the things that worry and disturb us. Instead of moving us toward self-improvement, excessive guilt is more likely to produce a sense of unworthiness that bogs us down.

The Twelve Step program provides tools for exposing and erasing guilt. We take inventory, which helps us to see where we have been wrong (and sometimes the wrong is simply in holding grudges and other bad feelings). We then share this with our sponsors and other close friends. They help us to bring our true problems into focus and to realize that we are still struggling with the ordinary shortcomings that are part of the human condition. We may be trying to live up to a perfection that is simply beyond our ability.

Then we release the problem to our Higher Power, who knows all and understands all. We are not always clear about the next steps we should take, but when we are sincerely trying to do our best, these usually become evident at the right time and in the right way.

This day I choose to accept full responsibility for my thoughts and actions, including acceptance of past wrongs. I know that God's forgiveness is within every situation and that my desire to follow the Twelve Step program leads me to higher and worthier actions.

March

DANGER IN EXCITEMENT

Mood Alterations The lure of excitement is hard to understand. While we may think of ourselves as sensible, practical people, the hard truth is that many alcoholics have a strong need to feel excited. This excitement can take many forms, and some of them are dangerous.

One lure of excitement comes through the impulsive need for change. Some of us have had weird habits of suddenly quitting jobs and pulling up stakes for no reason other than being bored. An even more destructive attraction is the belief that a new romance can restore our zest for living and bring new joys and happiness.

The sober truth is that nobody can live sensibly and sanely by seeking continuous excitement and stimulation. We are better off with steady growth in the patterns we know best than with seeking excitement that finally leads to destruction.

At the same time, we should not belittle the pleasures and joys we get through ordinary living. If we earn those pleasures and joys through responsible actions, they will give us far more happiness than momentary feelings of excitement.

In quietness and confidence is our strength. I do not need to be excited in any way today. I am more effective and more in control when I am not being swayed by feverish emotion that distorts my judgment.

DO WE NEED SOME FEAR?

Courage It's easy to get into an argument about the role of fear in our lives. Some say that we need *some* fear—it helps us get out of the path of an oncoming truck.

Is that really true? If it is, it's still not like the fear that was present with alcoholism. This fear was more likely to make us freeze and lose all power of action in the face of a threat. It was the sort of fear that paralyzes us, making us unable to move out of the way when a truck is bearing down on us.

Fear is even more destructive when it keeps us from doing the simple things we need to function in our lives. Fear certainly can't be helpful when it makes us unable to face a new customer or ride in an airplane for necessary business travel. Some people even put off medical examinations simply because they fear bad news—and thus delay treatment, so that their condition becomes worse.

We might not need to get rid of all fear, but we do need to dispose of the unhealthy kind that keeps us from necessary actions on our own behalf.

A really strong sense of the program can help me deal with fear today. One good idea for coping with fear is to remember that if God is for us, nobody can really be against us. Keeping that thought in mind can help stabilize our feelings in the face of threatening situations.

WHAT WILL THIS CHANGE BRING?

Change When facing *change*, it's not unusual to feel both apprehension and expectancy. We are apprehensive because we know that change includes risk. We feel expectancy, however, because we know that improvement can come only through some kind of change.

The way to handle change is to see it as part of the higher plan working in our lives. If we believe that our lives are in the care and keeping of our Higher Power, we have to know that everything is in good hands. As change occurs, it is simply part of a plan that is unfolding in order to bring more good into our lives.

We should not expect change without temporary disruptions or even surprises that appear to be setbacks. All that's necessary is to know that *change* is good if we maintain the right attitude toward it.

It's also helpful to review the past changes that have been so important in our lives. Once change has occurred, we come to accept it as normal, forgetting that it involved a lot of anxiety at one time. So it is with any change that is unfolding now. It's part of a wonderful plan that cannot fail.

I accept change without fear or superstition. Change is built into the nature of things, and will always be part of our lives. I accept it as readily as I accept the changes of the seasons.

DON'T FEED THE HABIT

Enhancing Sobriety We quickly learn that it's wrong to do anything that "feeds" a drinking habit. A recovering person would be foolish, for example, to spend time in a drinking environment simply to "be with friends."

It's constructive to take that same approach toward other problems we'd like to get out of our lives. If gossip has been my problem, for example, I should not feed it by listening to gossip or even by reading gossipy articles and books. If I have accumulated debts through overspending, I should cut off window shopping and other practices that may bring on more unnecessary debt. And if I want to rid my life of self-pity, I should not spend a single moment brooding over the bad breaks I have had in the past.

Bad habits have a life of their own. They are somewhat like rodents that have found their way into the house and have become star boarders. One way to control rodents is to eliminate their food supply. That same principle applies to bad habits we want to eliminate from our own lives.

I'll make a strong effort to cut off any line of thinking that feeds my bad habits, whatever they are. This might include avoiding practices that others see as harmless and trivial. However, nothing is harmless or trivial if it has become destructive in my life.

A VISION FOR YOU

A Positive Attitude One of the methods that helps in recovery is to see yourself as a sober person living a clean life. This is the "vision for you" that the society's founders offered in AA's early days, and it's still powerful today.

While being careful to avoid self-will, we can use this method with great success in living each day. Along with seeing ourselves sober, we can see ourselves living and working according to the best principles we know. We can see a business relationship improving. We can see some long-standing problems being solved. We can see a brighter side to negative situations that have persisted in spite of our best efforts to change them.

One author also talked about "seeing God on both sides of the table in any business negotiation." We desire success, of course, but it's also important to know that any negotiation ought to be successful for both parties. If we're really practicing spiritual principles in all of our affairs, there should be no desire to outmaneuver another person in any negotiation. There is always a price that is fair and satisfactory for both parties, and there are always terms suitable for both sides.

I will go through this day visualizing it as I think it should be according to the highest and best principles I know. I will put aside self-will and see everybody benefiting from any negotiation in which I am involved.

MARCH 6

EXAMPLE, NOT EXCEPTION

Helping Others   It's always heady stuff when others congratulate us on our victory over alcohol. Fair-minded people will have considerable admiration for what appears to be a bootstrap effort to make a comeback from despair and defeat.

We can accept this praise with grace and modesty. At some point, however, we should emphasize that our recovery was an example of spiritual principles at work and that thousands have been able to follow in the same path. Sober AA members are not exceptions; they are examples of what the program can do in people's lives.

It is important to emphasize that we are ordinary people. The marvelous thing about the program is that it works for ordinary people like ourselves. Many people in the fellowship have great talent and ability, but those gifts have nothing to do with staying sober. The gifted person gets sober the same way anybody does—by admitting powerlessness over alcohol and by accepting the program.

We are also helped most by people who can serve as examples in our lives. It is always inspiring to know that we can follow in their paths and find what has been given to them.

I want to provide a good example for others today. I will go through the day remembering that my sobriety is a gift that can be bestowed on anybody—it was not an exception just for me.

MARCH 7

FIRST THINGS FIRST

Order The struggle to bring order into our lives starts with lots of little things. One recovering person discovered that it was a good exercise simply to put the cap back on the toothpaste tube in the morning. This was a reminder that things should be put in their proper place, and the discipline helped later in organizing larger matters.

It is very easy to overlook orderly procedures in the haste to get things done, or to avoid anything that seems unpleasant or demanding. But such oversight always carries a heavy price later on. When we don't return things to their proper place, for example, we lose them or waste hours looking for them. We may bungle a job simply because we were too lazy to look up the right information or to read directions.

That's why "First things first" is much more than just a slogan. It's actually a principle for living, a guide that tells us there is an orderly approach to everything. If we can find that order without becoming slavishly compulsive about it, we'll find that it simplifies lots of things later on.

I'll try to do things in an orderly manner today. When I find myself taking short cuts or becoming too hurried, I'll regain control by remembering to establish priorities.

WHAT DO I PROJECT?

Personal Relations Were we ever told that our problems with other people really started within ourselves? If we have trouble getting along with another person, for example, is it because we are projecting mixed signals of fear and suspicion toward that person? We tend to reap what we sow—we get back the attitudes we project.

At the same time, however, we can't take total responsibility for the way others treat us or behave toward us. We cannot reform or control impossible people. When dealing with impossible people, we have control over our own feelings and responses. This helps us avoid potential trouble and enables us to deal with difficult situations.

But the principle of sowing what we reap—that is, getting back what we project—can really be proved by the person whose resentments and bitterness have driven away most of his or her friends. A simple change of attitude on our part can bring startling change for the better in the responses of others. With practice, the principle also applies to the broad area of human relations in many ways. For purposes of inventory, therefore, we should always look first at ourselves and our own thoughts and feelings when we find ourselves in a bad situation with others.

I will take care today to see that my thoughts and feelings toward others reflect what I want in my own life. I cannot expect to harbor secret resentments without getting some of my own back.

THE BEST OUTCOME
IS JUST AND EQUITABLE

Principle over Personality   Looking ahead to this day, I may face a possible conflict with another person over a certain issue. How should I respond to this?

If I'm to follow my principles, I should hold to the idea of *seeking the best outcome for everybody concerned.* It may be very harmful to look at these conflicts as a case of winning or losing. If I seem to win when I'm wrong, I will lose in the long run. If I seem to lose even when I'm right, I can know that there's a just resolution of everything in time. I will always win, however, if I keep my thinking straight and take care to avoid resentment and bitterness.

It's not surprising that the world is beset by conflicts. Millions of people have conditioned themselves to selfish ways of thinking and behaving that are bound to cause such conflicts. Much harm is done by people who are absolutely sure they are right at all times.

As human beings, we cannot expect to be excluded from these conflicts simply because we have a Twelve Step program. We do, however, have a means of dealing with such conflicts effectively when we respond according to principle. This makes us privileged people in a way, but it is good to know that any person can have the same privileges by following the right principles.

Unpleasant as any conflict may seem, it does give me an opportunity to learn and to grow. I will seek to benefit from any such conflict today.

OUSTING THE GREEN DEMON

Victory over Jealousy We hear of successful people who drop their old friends after moving up the ladder. Maybe, however, it wasn't their choice. Maybe they were driven to do so because their friends' jealousy made the friendship unworkable. We have little trouble accepting a stranger's good fortune; it's a different feeling, however, when friends and co-workers move ahead of us.

If the green demon of jealousy strikes during the day, we can come to terms with it in several ways. First, accept no guilt that it happens, because jealousy is part of the human condition. Next, depersonalize it by remembering that good fortune comes to all people in various ways. Then check your own gratitude level to make sure that it hasn't been sinking. This serves as a reminder that there's no shortage of the things that really make for happiness and personal well-being in life.

We can easily tell when we've been able to oust the green demon. We'll be able to be relaxed and gracious while extending congratulations for another person's good fortune. And months down the road, we'll be genuinely sympathetic—not vindictive—if the other person's luck turns sour.

While I don't expect to feel jealousy today, I accept the fact that it can happen. Should it appear, I'll work calmly to deal with it.

LIVING WITH BAD VIBES

Human Relations   Some of us are sensitive to the feelings we pick up from people in the immediate environment. The feelings we sense from the people around us can be as powerful as odors and sounds. We can feel tense in the presence of domineering people, and we can be uncomfortable around people who seem resentful.

Acceptance and knowledge help us retain mastery of ourselves in these situations. But we don't have to tune in to another person's bad feelings, just as we wouldn't tune in to a radio station whose music bothered us. We can also detach from the situation in thought, just as Al-Anon–trained spouses detach from alcoholics in a spirit of love and understanding.

The less we try to resist such a situation, the less power it has to disturb us. And the less involved we become with such situations, the sooner they seem to change. People in Twelve Step programs sometimes report miraculous changes when they adjust their own feelings. One frequently hears of outcomes such as this: "I learned not to let this person bother me, and two weeks later he was transferred to another department!"

My own sensitivity makes me vulnerable to good or bad feelings in the atmosphere. Recognizing them for what they are, I'll enjoy the good feelings and refuse to be disturbed or upset by those that seem bad.

POPULAR GOSSIP

Higher Thinking   The newsstands are full of publications that seem to delight in exposing the sins and foibles of celebrities and prominent officials. Think of the excitement that's been generated just over the sexual misadventures of important people running for public office.

While some of these disclosures may be true, we don't help ourselves by reveling in them or reading them. We may even harm ourselves if we get secret enjoyment over the fall of a celebrity. It's never beneficial to find ourselves thinking, "It serves him right!"

Reading such trash, even in the daily newspapers, is a form of gossip. We can use our time in better ways if we wish to enhance our sobriety.

If this sounds a little too stringent, we should remind ourselves that growth in sobriety calls for better management of our thinking and attitudes. Nobody ever got drunk simply because he or she read gossipy trash. But neither did that person make progress over the general problem of gossip.

I'll have no interest in the weaknesses or shortcomings of those who might be in the news. Popular gossip can be just as harmful as personal gossip.

MARCH 13

BELIEVING IN JUSTICE

Justice "What goes around, comes around," is a popular saying. It's often used to suggest that certain arrogant, unprincipled people will eventually receive their comeuppance. It conveys the idea that there's a hidden justice at work in human affairs that assures all injustice will eventually be punished.

But if it works to punish, this hidden justice also rewards right actions, and this is more important in our working of the program. If we act from good motives, we'll always find that our work is rewarded in some way. No alcoholic who performs a service in the fellowship goes unrewarded. Quite often the reward is simply a personal sense of well-being and growth in character, but these may be more important than money or recognition.

Justice is one of the cardinal virtues—a Godlike attribute that human beings strive to understand. Believing in justice is believing in the Hidden Power that orders justice in all things.

I'll view my world today as something that is controlled and ordered by a Just Power. Reward and retribution are built into the scheme of things, but I'll focus more on actions that bring the right kinds of rewards.

LIVING WITH DEPRESSION

Mood Management   Getting sober is often only a first small step in getting well. Many recovering alcoholics must also face an underlying depression that seems to mock their efforts to attain real serenity. But sobriety does not cause the depression. It simply lays bare a condition that was present all along, but had been masked by repeated binges. It's probably true, too, that many of us used alcohol partly as a drug to combat depression because it temporarily lifted our mood and relieved our pain.

One fact about depression is that it comes and goes; we can endure it partly by knowing that "this too shall pass." Another fact is that physical activity helps in coping with it. AA cofounder Bill W., victimized by profound depression even in his sober years, found that walking provided some relief, though he had to force himself to do it at times. A third fact about depression is that we can usually alleviate its effects by helping others and by staying close to AA circles, even when we're too depressed to contribute much. It's also helpful to discuss the problem with understanding friends and sponsors, or a therapist, if necessary.

I'll believe today that I can maintain a good mood level that continues to build as I carry out my responsibilities and make AA first in my life. Depression may challenge me, but I don't have to give in to it.

THE SECRET OF DETACHMENT

Dealing with Others "Detaching with love" is what those close to alcoholics do when they realize they can't change them. The same principle should apply to any distressing situation, but how does it work? How can I detach from people who really bother me—especially fellow workers, or perhaps a boss or customer?

The secret of detachment is expressed in the biblical charge, "Resist not evil." We don't fight or resist the other person, or even try to change another's behavior. We stop believing that the other person's behavior can really control us in the future. We become impersonal about something that was once highly charged with resentment and bitterness. At no point, however, do we say that the others' wrong behavior is all right, nor do we lie to ourselves about what the other is doing.

Detachment does not mean that the outcome will be recovery or change for the other person. That sometimes happens, and we're grateful when it does. If we detach in the right way, however, the outcome will always be better than anything we could bring about by fighting the situation. We have to count an outcome favorable if we stay sober and under control in the midst of an insane situation.

I will detach myself from conflicts with others if they arise today. I am not going to fight anything or anybody, and I know this will bring me closer to the ideal of living at peace with everybody.

ANGER—A DANGEROUS WEAPON

Self-Control One reason some of us have trouble overcoming anger is that we've used it too often as an offensive weapon. It can be employed as an excuse to leave the house, it can bring an argument to an explosive end, and it can make others fearful and defensive. In the past this brought results of a sort, and helped reinforce the idea that anger works.

The trouble with anger, though, is that it's destructive. Once angry, we hurt ourselves and we hurt others. Terrible things said in anger leave wounds that never heal, creating problems that lead to more anger.

The AA program can show us that there is virtually no justification for anger, under any and all circumstances. If we sense it coming on, we have the choice of taking charge of our feelings. If we're angry over another's behavior, we can choose to practice acceptance. Above all, we can remember that anger might be a way of reacting, but it's not necessary in our lives.

I'll make it through this day without a trace of anger. I'll frequently remind myself that anger is destructive and that my real purpose is to build a better life.

IS IT EASY?

Practicing Principles There's no "softer, easier way," we're told. If so, why are we also urged to embrace the slogan "Easy does it"? Which is right?

Both are right, because they express two different ideas. The softer, easier way *doesn't work* because it grows out of self-deception and falls short of a thorough working of the program. "Easy does it" *works* because it describes an approach to action that is relaxed, confident, and careful.

The person seeking an easier, softer way usually avoids taking some of the steps that are considered necessary in maintaining sobriety. It's a way of trying to win without doing sufficient work. The person following the "Easy does it" principle pays attention to every detail, but carries on without reasonable haste or excessive loafing.

In a spiritual sense, "Easy does it" also means letting the Higher Power carry the load. At all times, however, we must continue to make choices and bear responsibility for our actions.

I'll be relaxed and confident while carrying on a full day's activity. There is always time to do things the right way.

SHOULD EVERYBODY LIKE ME?

Personal Relations   In AA discussions, the term *people-pleaser* doesn't fare very well. When people say they are people-pleasers, they're acknowledging that it's also a problem.

It's a problem because it reflects a desire to have everybody's acceptance and approval—to be universally liked. But from what we know about human relationships, this is not possible. No matter how hard we work to be pleasant and likable, some people may still detest us for reasons we cannot understand. When that happens, we should not blame ourselves or step up our efforts to win them over. Our best course is to be cordial to them and to avoid giving offense in any way, while accepting the fact that they do not like us.

If our own behavior is mature and reasonable, even the people who don't like us will at least respect us. That may be the best we can hope for, and it is certainly far better than shameless people pleasing. In the end, people-pleasers don't please anybody and, as a famous comedian notes about himself, they "get no respect."

I'll try hard to be pleasant and cordial to everyone I meet today. If some people do not respond in the same way, I'll accept this without feeling hurt or betrayed.

WHERE IS GOD?

Guidance AA members have always had a difficult time explaining the "God business." We didn't want to be considered religious, but at the same time we've always believed some contact with a Higher Power is necessary for real personal growth.

There's nothing wrong—for our purposes—in simply visualizing God as a Higher Power that has always been *within us and around us.* "Before they call, I will answer," goes an old saying, and that was true even in our darkest days. Many of us can look back to realize that a certain force was moving us toward recovery long before we knew we needed any recovery. Many of us also believe that a Higher Power helped bring AA into being and move it along to become a worldwide force for good.

But God works in ways that can seem to come from chance or coincidence. Quite often, we'll find that little events had far-reaching results in our lives. When we review how such things happened, we should not conclude that this happens only to certain "special" people. All human beings are part of God's creation and can avail themselves of guidance and direction. The more serious problem is that guidance and direction are sometimes ignored or rejected.

I'll go about my affairs today with the knowledge that my Higher Power is making the important decisions in my life. I'll come out about where God wants me to be.

THINK, THINK, THINK

Prudence It's hard to believe, but some AA members insist that newcomers shouldn't think. "Whoever said you should think?" some members are told. The newcomer is apparently supposed to suspend all thinking for several months until reaching a certain level of recovery.

This is nonsense, and it also contradicts AA teaching. If we don't want people to use their heads, why do we have printed cards on meeting room walls that say, "Think, Think, Think"? We are always capable of thinking, even in moments of deep despair. Indeed, we could not keep from thinking.

A constructive approach to thinking is to form complete sentences from the slogan on the wall: *Think* what might happen if I take one drink. *Think* of the wonderful new life that awaits me in sobriety. *Think* about ways of improving myself and following a more satisfactory lifestyle.

It's also important to remember that good thinking will drive out bad thinking—but good thinking has to be cultivated.

I'll keep my thinking centered today on the good things that can be done in life. I'll focus my attention only on matters that are under my control, and I know that better thinking will bring better conditions.

LIVING ONE DAY AT A TIME

Time Management   It's surprising that some alcoholics learn how to "live one day at a time" while drinking. It had to work that way, or their drinking life would have been even more intolerable. It was convenient to shut off thoughts of tomorrow if one had enough money to drink today. It was also convenient to blot out thoughts of yesterday, which only meant remorse.

In sobriety, living one day at a time is an excellent way to focus our minds so we can pour our energies into the work at hand. In reviewing the wasted yesterdays, we can always find ways that we could have been more productive and effective. But we missed opportunities because we were still struggling with regrets or fearing what might happen in the future.

It's never too late to change all that. We need neither regret the past nor fear the future. The AA secret is to make the best of today's challenges. It may mean just chipping away at a massive problem that seems insurmountable. Living just for today, we can do today's job well.

I'll live comfortably and happily in the here and now. This means releasing the past and accepting the future as something I'll deal with at the proper time.

LET GO AND LET GOD

Guidance Though it came from outside AA, the idea of "letting go and letting God" has taken root in the fellowship. The trouble comes when we try to decide what it really means. We obviously need to continue working and we still have to make important decisions. So how do we let God take charge?

Surrendering to God's will is a shift that takes place in our attitude. We take whatever actions seem reasonable and proper according to our view of things. We remember, however, that a better plan may be unfolding in every situation. In many cases, it can even be a case of wanting too little rather than too much. One member, for example, sought guidance in a business decision. He was disappointed when the deal fell through, but discovered, only a few weeks later, an even better opportunity that worked out perfectly.

"Letting God" is really a form of working Step Eleven—seeking "knowledge of His will for us and the power to carry that out." As we do that, our lives must become enriched and improved in every way.

I'll approach the day with the idea that God is working it out for the highest good of everybody. Temporary setbacks won't bother me if I know that God's plan is unfolding in my life.

ACT AS IF

Finding Direction Though it sounds like a game or a trick, there's great power in "acting as if." This means acting as if we've already succeeded, acting as if we expect everybody to cooperate with us, acting as if we've already reached whatever goal we're seeking.

The principle behind this approach is that such acting helps focus our minds and energies on goals. It's also important to believe that our success is inevitable if we are truly on the right path.

We should not employ this principle superstitiously or assume it's a substitute for intelligent work and good judgment. It will be a substantial aid, however, in helping us eliminate the self-doubt and pessimism that dog so many alcoholics during their quest for sobriety. Too often, low self-esteem and a faulty belief that nothing will turn out right have led us to sabotage our own efforts.

We should go into any venture with the idea that we've already succeeded—that much good is going to come out of it, even if the exact outcome is somewhat different from what we had in mind. "Acting as if" is just what we might need to summon our powers for the duties ahead.

An old saying affirms that "if God be for me, who can be against me?" I'll carry on today with the confidence that my Higher Power is guiding all my efforts in the right direction.

THIS TOO SHALL PASS

Fortitude Growing older in sobriety, we soon become aware of the fact that both good and bad experiences eventually pass on. No matter how beautiful or ugly a situation becomes, it must change in time. In discussions, we catch this idea by reminding ourselves that "this too shall pass."

We are very fortunate that this is true. Were it otherwise, intolerable conditions would last forever. Our business is to make sure that our own thoughts and actions lead to betterment, for ourselves and others. While we should be willing to accept unpleasantness if there is no way of avoiding it, we should always hope—and work—for improvement.

When unpleasant experiences do pass on, we must also be careful not to resurrect them by brooding about how badly we were treated or trying to get even with others. This only prolongs the trouble. The good news in AA is that we can survive any experience and put it behind us.

Whatever I'm facing today, I'll know that it is temporary and has no power to keep me from the deeper happiness and gratitude I have in the Twelve Step program.

EXPECT MIRACLES

Belief   Some have claimed that there have been no miracles since the fourteenth century. This is a smug way of saying that miracles do not happen.

Emmet Fox conceded that miracles don't happen in the sense of violating the perfect, universal system of law and order. But there is such a thing as appealing to a higher law, and this too is part of the constitution of the universe. Prayer is a means of doing this, and enough prayer will get you out of any difficulty, Fox insisted.

People who have found sobriety in AA are actually modern miracles. They expect more miracles to continue happening; otherwise, there would be no point in continuing to work with newcomers. And while we're expecting miracles, let's remember that countless other human problems will yield to a spiritual approach. Life itself is miraculous when we study it; why shouldn't there be more miracles ahead?

I'll keep an open mind on the subject of miracles. Since we still can glimpse only a fragment of the universe, it should follow that there's also much more to learn about the spiritual processes that rescued us from alcoholism.

I CAN'T . . . GOD CAN . . .
I THINK I'LL LET GOD

Guidance One of the delusions that keep alcoholics in bondage is the belief in the power of the personal will. "I still think I'm strong enough to whip it," alcoholics have declared defiantly, just before heading out for another debacle.

Willpower has a role in recovery, but only in making a decision to turn the problem over to Higher Power. This sets in motion powerful forces that come to our assistance. We don't know how and why this process works as it does. We do know that it has worked repeatedly for those who sincerely apply it in their lives.

What's needed to start the process is an admission of defeat, a willingness to seek a Higher Power, and at least enough open-mindedness to give it all a fair chance. The outcome can be very surprising.

There's also no need to be apologetic about our Higher Power after we've found sobriety. Nobody had a better plan, and we can remember that other severe problems can be handled in the same way.

I'll do my best today to solve every problem and meet every responsibility. If something is too much for me, I'll turn it over in the same way I did my drinking problem.

IF IT WORKS, DON'T FIX IT

Accepting Life   A lot of things in life are all right just as they are. This is hard to understand in a world that puts high value on improvement and progress, but since there are so many things that do need fixing, it's best not to tamper with things that are working.

Sometimes we think something should be changed in another person's life. Two AA members decided, for example, that a mutual AA friend deserved higher status employment than what he was doing. They seized upon an unusual profession that seemed to fit his talents and interests, and were disappointed and even a bit offended when he decided he wasn't interested. He continued to follow his regular trade until his retirement thirty years later.

In truth, there had really been nothing that needed "fixing" in his choice of a vocation. He had been earning a living doing very honest but difficult work. It was somewhat presumptuous of his friends to outline a new career for him, and it could have led to considerable harm.

Let's leave people and things alone unless our help is requested and something really does need fixing.

I'll look around today and notice the things in my life that are working well and really don't need changing. Then I'll focus my attention on the things that really should be fixed.

KEEP COMING BACK—
IT WORKS IF YOU WORK IT

Fortitude   A popular self-help book noted that there is tremendous power in repetition—like the tap-tap-tap of a hammer that finally drives the nail through a board. AA works in much the same way; attendance at meetings is the steady tap-tap-tap that helps bring about lasting sobriety and personal improvement.

Attending meetings is also much like attending school. Nobody learns everything in one classroom session, and it's also true that the student must put forth an effort to learn.

We should accept AA as something that will gradually grow on us if we become part of it and apply ourselves to its principles. The willingness to continue attending meetings is some evidence of sincerity and commitment. We discover that there are few meetings that bring us world-shaking revelations and experiences, but as we keep coming back and working the program, our own lives will improve steadily. This is the result of many meetings, not just a few.

I'll do everything possible today to strengthen my sobriety and my understanding of the program. Rather than seeking shortcuts, I'll be grateful for steady progress.

MARCH 29

STICK WITH THE WINNERS

Making the Right Choices In the world of drinking, people lead each other down paths of further destruction. In the world of AA, that same destructive process can still go on through wrong thinking. It's possible for AA members to encourage resentments, criticism, gossip, and other dead-end practices.

That's why people are urged to "stick with the winners" in order to find and maintain sobriety. Seek out people who are doing well in the program, people whose progress is noticeable and admirable. They can be of real help as sponsors, as friends, or simply as role models.

It's important to remember that the winners can be from all walks of life. The first AA member in Detroit earned only a modest living, while the second Detroit member became a wealthy manufacturer after finding sobriety. In AA terms, both men were winners. They stayed sober, they stayed active in the fellowship, and they helped others.

"Sticking with the winners" does not mean we should shun people who are having difficulty with the program. It does mean we should avoid accepting ideas and ways of living that do not lead to sobriety.

I'll spend time in the company of people who have a good record of following the program.

MARCH 30

IDENTIFY, DON'T COMPARE

Good Judgment There's always danger in comparing ourselves with others. If we use behavior and drinking as yardsticks, such comparisons can lead us to believe that we might not really be alcoholics. This mistaken conclusion has been the undoing of some alcoholics.

The better course is to *identify* with the problems others have *in common* with us. Though drinking patterns and habits may vary between two people, individuals may at least share the fears and delusions that drinking brought.

Other common factors that bind alcoholics together are emotional immaturity, a misplaced faith that alcohol solves problems, loneliness, and a tendency toward resentments. These also make good discussion topics for meetings.

At the very beginning of AA, the founders had trouble coming up with a real definition of alcoholism. Since then, we've done very well by letting members "diagnose" themselves. It's best to leave it this way: If your drinking is a problem in your life, AA has an answer for you.

Today I will not waste time comparing myself with others. Having accepted my alcoholism, I'll devote my attention to the things that enhance sobriety.

A JOURNEY, NOT A DESTINATION

How It Works "Now that you're sober, why do you stay in AA?" AA members frequently hear this from others not familiar with the fellowship, but it's understandable. They see AA as a place where one goes to be "cured," whereas we learn to see it as an ongoing recovery process that is never really completed.

Sobriety is not an object that one can acquire and then put on a shelf somewhere or on the wall like a diploma. It is more of a journey in living, with each day's march being a goal in itself.

You could also say that sobriety is like the "manna from heaven" described in the Old Testament. Fresh manna arrived each day, but could not be saved for the future. It is the same with us. Today's experience in sobriety is what sustains us, and we're in trouble if we're trying to depend on what was accomplished in the past.

Though we do use the term *permanent sobriety*, we never truly possess it. Our quest for sobriety is a lifetime journey.

I'll be on guard against any feeling of "having it made." Sure, past success should be helpful in maintaining today's sobriety. But the quality of today's sobriety will depend only on today's thinking and behavior.

April

THERE ARE NO COINCIDENCES

Guidance   Here's an exercise that can strengthen your belief in a Higher Power: Review your life for seemingly insignificant things that were actually major turning points. A chance meeting, for example, may have resulted in an astonishing career opportunity or lifelong romance. Such surprises come to everybody, and people often wonder what their lives would have been like without these "coincidences."

The founding of AA also seemed to be a series of coincidences and chance happenings. The message reached Bill W. by a circular route, and then an unexpected business opportunity took him to Akron, Ohio, where he finally met Dr. Bob. The unusual aspect was that Akron just "happened" to have stalwart members of the Oxford Group, the same fellowship that had helped Bill W.

People with strong spiritual foundations in AA have come to see these happenings not as coincidences but as the guidance of a Higher Power. This Higher Power was—and is—continuously working through inspired people.

We'll find similar chance happenings for good in our own lives. We don't control them except by keeping our own house in order. This assures us that the outcome of any "coincidence" will be favorable.

I'll carry on my activities today without trying to second-guess what my Higher Power has in mind for me. At the same time, I'll know that a superior intelligence is directing my affairs in wonderful ways.

ACCEPTING RISK

Facing Reality Like it or not, life seems to have certain risks that just can't be avoided. Alcoholics are not really comfortable with risk-taking. This is especially true in situations that include risk of rejection, risk of defeat, or risk of loss.

If we try to get through life without accepting some risk, however, we're simply not being realistic. The refusal to accept risk may also mean that we miss wonderful opportunities in the process.

What should we do? We should face risk intelligently and with spiritual preparation. First, we do everything possible to reduce risk in any situation (thus making it a "calculated" risk). Then we pray for guidance and inspiration (but not a certain outcome). Finally, we do our very best to succeed in the situation, whether it's a courtship, a job search, competition in sports, or whatever.

We might surprise ourselves by succeeding more times than we fail. But even in temporary failure, we gain if we followed through in accepting reasonable and necessary risks.

I'll exercise prudence and good judgment in all my undertakings today, but I won't expect to be able to "play it safe" in everything. As a human being, I have to take risks in life.

MORE WILL BE REVEALED

Spiritual Growth   There's an old saying, "To him that hath, more shall be given." That saying applies to our growth in AA. If we dedicate ourselves to the program, new information and understanding will continue to flow in our direction.

This is not because God is singling us out for special favors. It's simply a law of life. When we are interested in a subject, we find more knowledge coming to us almost "out of the blue" as we continue to seek it. It's almost as if hidden forces were gathering up ideas and pushing them in our direction.

What's happened is that we have put ourselves in line for such growth. We have our antennae out, and we become conditioned to recognize useful ideas as they come to us. We are open-minded to our good.

This same process has also led to more general knowledge about alcoholism. When the early AAs attained sobriety, most of the information about alcoholism was summed up in a handful of books. Now there are hundreds of books, symposia, and speeches dealing with the subject. More was revealed, and we can hope that even more will be revealed as we continue to focus on recovery.

I can expect useful information to come to me from a number of sources. My interest in my recovery and self-improvement helps attract the information and understanding I need.

YOU ARE NOT ALONE

Fellowship If you feel isolated and lonely, tape the letters YANA to the dash of your car. "*You Are Not Alone*" can help bring a surge of confidence when you most need it.

We are not alone because we have thousands of friends who have shared our experience and who understand our feelings. We also are not alone because we have a Higher Power who presides over the affairs of all humankind. We can never be separated from this Power except in our own minds.

We must remember that we will always *need* other people. Virtually everything that benefits us is supplied by the skills and knowledge of others. We can believe that we are completely independent, but the truth is that no person survives completely alone.

The typical problem for many of us is in failing to seek help from others. If extreme loneliness is closing in on us, the best prescription is a meeting and the company of other members.

I'll not be too proud to ask for help today or to explain to others that I need them and appreciate them. I should also freely admit that help from others led me to sobriety—and helps maintain it today.

LETTING GO OF RESENTMENT

Releasing the Past   How can we *really* put an end to festering resentments toward other people? "Pray for these people," the Old-Timers said. "Go out of your way to do something good for them." This is a big order for most of us, but we are working for a big reward: sobriety, peace of mind, and personal progress.

When we pray for others in this manner, we're practicing the noble art of forgiveness. How do we know when it's starting to work? Lewis B. Smedes, a master teacher of forgiveness, offers this thought: "You will know that forgiveness has begun when you recall those who hurt you and feel the power to wish them well."

Forgiveness also is supposed to include forgetting the wrong. What we really forget is the hurt connected with it. When anything that once evoked pain comes to mind, we're growing spiritually if it no longer has the power to hurt us.

We then discover that we had been letting our resentments hurt us again and again. We also learn that one effort to forgive is not nearly enough. Forgiveness takes the same amount of practice and emotional power we put into carrying the resentment!

Today will bring enough problems. I don't have either the time or the energy to play the old tapes that cause me pain. I'll practice praying for those who hurt me, and I'll take it for granted that my Higher Power is removing my resentments.

THE BARRIER OF SICK PRIDE

Sharing Feelings Pride can be either sick or healthy. It's *sick* pride that keeps us in bondage to alcohol. It's *healthy* pride that emerges when we have high self-esteem. Finding the right path in sobriety always involves a battle to keep sick pride out of our lives.

What if I'm at a discussion meeting and I feel reluctant to admit that certain character defects are still giving me trouble? Can this be sick pride carrying on the pretense that I have risen above such problems? What if someone takes issue with a point I've tried to make in a discussion? Does sick pride cause me to react in self-defense?

We learn in the Twelve Step program that we gain nothing by attempting to conceal our character defects from our fellow members. We gain everything by sharing our true feelings and letting others know we are vulnerable human beings. There is never any need to defend or explain anything we've tried to say in a meeting. The real message always comes through in our attitude, and it will reach those for whom it's intended.

I'll check myself today to see if sick pride is dictating what I say and do. The more I can let others see me as I really am, the more honest my relationships will be.

DESERVING HAPPINESS

Emotional Control Somewhere in the course of living sober, we should realize that we can *deserve* to be happy. If happiness is eluding us, the fault may lie in a peculiar guilt from our past. In a perverse way, we may be using unhappiness as penance for our past wrongs.

We deserve to be happy if we are doing the things that should bring happiness to ourselves and others. Thinking and living rightly is a path to happiness. Meeting our obligations to society and others contributes to personal happiness. Placing the overall responsibility for our lives in God's hands is yet another route to happiness.

We can also learn from our experience. Did any of us ever meet a truly happy person who was totally self-seeking? Do we remember any happy, serene people among our drinking companions? Did any of our temporary successes and victories bring permanent happiness?

AA experience gives us the answers we need. Happiness is always in the direction of love and service, never in anything selfish. We deserve to be happy, but we must plant seeds of happiness by our thoughts and actions.

I'll be happy today. If I'm worrying about something, I'll suspend the worry and let myself be happy in spite of it. I deserve to be happy and I am usually the person who is responsible for this happiness.

KEEP IT SIMPLE,
BUT NOT SIMPLE-MINDED

Working the Steps   Dr. Bob Smith left little in the way of written material for AA's future. His phrase "Keep it simple," however, is now a guiding slogan in the program. What did he really have in mind with this final piece of advice?

We can take it as certain that Dr. Bob—a highly intelligent man—was not saying that we shouldn't use our heads for real thinking and study. One of the blessings of sobriety, in fact, should be the ability to think clearly and effectively. It would be a mistake to believe that one must renounce brainpower and education in order to stay sober.

The real aim of "keeping it simple" should be to stay mindful of the principles and essentials that are key to everything else. Even the most difficult subjects can usually be mastered by processes of simplification. The deepest book, for example, is still composed of only twenty-six letters.

We can "keep it simple" by building our lives around the principles of the Twelve Step program. When we discover new ideas, they'll reinforce and expand what we've already learned. In this way, we should always be learning and growing—which is beautifully simple, but certainly not simple-minded.

I'll be grateful today for the ability to think and to understand complicated subjects. With a strong foundation in the bedrock principles of AA, I can use my mind in constructive and progressive ways.

UNDERSTANDING COMPULSION

Protecting Sobriety Often called a "compulsive illness," alcoholism is still a baffling mystery to most people. All we really know is that a single drink, a pleasant beverage for many, becomes a deadly trigger for alcoholics. We may even think it's unfair that we're unable to enjoy the pleasant customs of social drinking. If we let down our guard, we can even entertain the thought that we've somehow been cured of the compulsion to drink.

But we don't have to understand the exact nature of compulsion to realize that we are victims of it. Bitter experience and the tragic examples of others should tell us that our compulsion exists and is activated by the first drink. That's really all the understanding we need for living successfully in sobriety.

If there's anything we should question, it's not whether we have the compulsion, but why we would have any doubts after so much bad experience with alcohol. After all, if we always had a bad reaction from any other food or beverage, we would soon give it up. Why is there so much persistence in denying that we are compulsively attached to alcohol?

We still may be trying to convince ourselves that we can take a drink safely, and this delusion is another way the compulsion works. All we have to understand is that a single drink leads to our destruction.

I'll remember today that I've accepted the fact that I am alcoholic and subject to disaster with a first drink. I'll live today with the knowledge that I only have to understand that I have the compulsion to drink.

WALK IN DRY PLACES

Protecting Sobriety   Though AA members never criticize drinking customs, we do tell newcomers that it's wise to avoid situations involving alcohol. Even this is not an absolute, because we also concede that it's sometimes necessary to attend a cocktail reception or to lunch with a friend in a bar. So how do we distinguish between what's safe and what's likely to lead to trouble?

The litmus test is always to look at our own motives and spiritual guidance. A drink has no power over us unless we *want* to take the drink. If we are not deliberately seeking out drinking situations, our motives are probably good. If our spiritual house is in order, our Higher Power will also protect us in any situation.

Wherever we go, however, we should also make our sobriety the first priority of business. Whatever the importance of any social event, it is insignificant compared with the importance of sobriety. Keep sobriety at the top of your list, and the other decisions will follow in proper order.

We should hold the additional thought that "walking in dry places" is really thinking of ourselves as always being in dry places under God's guidance.

Today I will focus on the sober world I want to enjoy and share. The world of drinking has nothing for me. I may encounter situations involving casual drinking today, but I will not be part of them in mind and spirit. I will think and walk in dry places.

HELPING OTHERS

Motives It may sound selfish, but you should always help others for no reason other than your own benefit. In giving assistance, guard against posing as an idealist or even a Good Samaritan. We are not saints, and our spiritual progress is interrupted the moment we begin to act more saintly than we really are.

Two things happen when we help others in the full knowledge that we are really helping only ourselves. First, we do not place the other person in a demeaning role or make him or her obligated to us. Second, we sidestep the swollen egotism that could arise if we view ourselves as rescuers.

In helping others, we are only passing on the good that has come to us. Any good action will always bring rich rewards in personal well-being. People we have helped will be grateful to us when it becomes clear that we don't demand their gratitude. They will also be inspired to follow this example, which is the true AA spirit that became evident with the first Twelve Step calls.

I'll look for opportunities to help others in the same way that a businessman looks for ways to increase profits. I know that I grow as a person when I help others in the right spirit.

APRIL 12

BEATING DEPRESSION

Emotional Fortitude If you're seeking a lively meeting discussion topic, bring up depression. It's so closely tied to alcoholism that some people even think alcoholics are attempting to "treat" depression when they drink. Others feel that depression shows they're not "working" the program.

Overcoming depression is a monumental undertaking, but that doesn't mean it cannot be done. The deadly mistake is to believe your circumstances are so hopeless that there's no solution. Sometimes, as AA cofounder Bill Wilson contended (based on personal experience), depression actually corrects itself in time. Stay sober, live rightly, keep physically and mentally active, and in time some depressive mood swings will ease. Even more serious clinical depression can be treated.

It's human to be temporarily depressed about a terrible failure or setback. The Twelve Steps are tools for coping with unpleasant situations, but we still might feel bad about them for a time. The really good news is that enough fortitude will see us through for the long term. We have much experience to show that this is true.

Whether today's mood is up or down, I'll hold to the view that the Twelve Steps will help me defeat mental depression in time. My Higher Power assures me that joy and peace are my rightful state of mind.

APRIL 13

NO CONDITIONAL SOBRIETY

Admission of Powerlessness Sobriety in AA is unconditional. This means that there's never been a reason for drinking, no matter how bad our circumstances may become. As the AA pioneers were fond of saying, "There's nothing that drinking won't make worse."

How do we know if we've been setting conditions on sobriety? It's revealed to us in our own thinking. If we believe, for example, that a certain setback such as the ending of a relationship is just cause for drinking, we have made our sobriety conditional.

In such cases, what we need to do is clear up our own thinking on the subject. Maybe further inventory is needed, or perhaps we should let ourselves learn from the experience of others. Self-honesty is also important in getting priorities in order.

The decision to choose unconditional sobriety brings additional benefits in helping us to organize our lives. Once we completely understand that sobriety is all-important, it becomes easier to make other decisions that bear on keeping sober. We find ourselves choosing the ideas and activities that enhance sobriety, while rejecting other things that could threaten it.

I'll never waver in a moment from my belief that I must continue to seek sobriety—unconditionally. There is nothing that could ever justify my taking a drink.

WHAT CAUSES A BINGE?

Understanding Honesty In the foggy world of drinking, we were sometimes confused about cause and effect. A person might think of a binge as having been caused by a fight with his or her spouse. The real truth, however, is that he or she provoked the fight in order to get out of the house to launch a drinking spree. It was really the need to drink that caused the fight, and not the reverse, as the alcoholic believes.

We must always understand that the compulsion to drink is the root cause of every binge. We may blame certain things that seemed to trigger a drunk, but it is always our own compulsion that gives force to such an action. Nonalcoholics have the same human experiences we do, but such things do not cause them to have binges.

Seasoned AA members are trained by their experience to detect and defuse these false causes. "There are excuses but never good reasons for drinking," they say. We always drink because we *want* to drink, not because another's actions forced us into it.

Once we've established real sobriety, we also learn to identify the excuses and devices that helped us blame our binges on other people and conditions. We learn that we are always responsible for maintaining our own sobriety.

I intend to get along with everybody today and to meet all conditions and circumstances in a mature manner. Nothing can trigger a binge but my own desire to take a drink.

WHEN THINGS ARE NOT
HUMANLY POSSIBLE

Facing Difficulties We're reminded again and again that "no human power could have relieved our alcoholism." Whatever it is that keeps us sober must come from a Higher Power—God as we understand [God].

This fact about our alcoholism also has broader application to the general conditions of life. There's an almost endless list of conditions that are not humanly possible to change. Some of these conditions apply only to us; others, such as war and disease, cruelly afflict all of humankind. Looking at this sorry picture, many of us wish we had the power to apply Twelve Step principles to *all* human problems.

While we don't have such power at the moment, we do have the power to take a spiritual view of all seemingly hopeless conditions. This includes trying to do whatever we can about any problem, while recognizing that the real solution must eventually come from a Higher Power. We must never lose hope that God will work with us and through us to create a better world. In a small way, we can help by sharing what happened to us in our recovery from alcoholism. No human power could have relieved our alcoholism, but God could and did.

Though I live and work with people who may be frightened and cynical, I'll hold to the idea that a Higher Power is working ceaselessly to improve the human condition in general. There is no reason why the miraculous healing power that relieved my alcoholism should not apply to other problems in my life.

FIX THE NEED

Taking Inventory Recovering users have a saying: "Need a fix? Fix the need!" It's great advice, if we combine it with our daily inventory.

In good behavior and bad, we're always trying to meet our needs. As compulsive people, we have lots of experience with destructive ways of meeting them. Driven by nameless hungers, we tried desperately to combat boredom, to raise our low self-esteem, to find companionship. What we actually did was place more distance between ourselves and the true satisfying of our needs.

On the new path, one way of fixing needs is to come to terms with them. Maybe we had a need for success that was really a frantic effort to "show others" that we were all right. We should want to succeed, but let's begin by exchanging any false goal for one that's right for us. Maybe we have other needs that are based on defective principles and immature hopes.

What do we really need? All of us need self-honesty, self-worth, friendship, and purpose—all available in the AA program as part of sober living. Finding these, we'll gain insight that will enable us to sort out and understand other needs—and perhaps find those that correspond to our heart's desire and bring real happiness. It's something we can turn over, because God knows our needs before we even ask.

I'll remember today that my needs exist to serve my way of life, and that I must never be a slave to them.

WE CAN'T GO HOME AGAIN

Living Here and Now   Despite all evidence that we must live for today, some of us persist in trying to recapture the past. We may be holding a few good memories that we would like to bring alive today. More likely, we may also be refighting old battles in the hope that this time we'll come out winners.

But since change is taking place everywhere at every moment, we can never return to any previous place or time. Time does march on, and we are part of the parade. Whether we were winners or losers in the past, we can live only in the here and now.

The good news is that we can retain any lessons from the past and put them to use today. If we have scalding memories of twisted relationships, we can remind ourselves that growth and understanding now place us out of harm's way. And if we remember the things that did turn out right even in the confused past, we can reflect that even greater good is possible today.

Our home is never in the past. It is in the time and place where we are today. As we make the best of it, all of our future homes in place and time will improve, for "in God's house are many mansions."

Accepting the value of all of its lessons, I will close the door firmly on the past, knowing that I must devote all of my interest and energies to the present moment.

MISTAKES ARE FOR LEARNING

Personal Growth One sign of an alcoholic's immaturity is revealed in responses to personal mistakes. We take each simple mistake as further proof of our inadequacy. As one woman observed, "I can handle a general catastrophe, but running my nylons can ruin my day."

Some of us may feel we're victims of past conditioning—a parent, for example, who berated us when the slightest thing went wrong. But we're at fault if we continue to let ourselves be victimized by such experience. We should give no person—past, present, or future—the right to set the level of our self-esteem.

Properly viewed, all mistakes are for learning purposes. We often have to make a few mistakes before we can learn anything. Sometimes a mistake can occur simply to teach us one basic lesson—that we are human and cannot be perfect in everything we do.

Above all, we should never condemn ourselves for the countless mistakes that occurred while we were drinking. Our alcoholism, a terrible mistake in the sight of many, led to the deep learning we find in AA. Nothing that brings us this far can really be a mistake in the sight of God.

In sobriety, I'm learning to tolerate the shortcomings and mistakes of others. I will extend the same grace to myself today if I make a simple mistake.

WHO PUSHES MY BUTTONS?

Personal Relations   AA old-timers would be mystified today to hear program members talk about people "pushing their buttons." This expression wasn't around when the early AA members pulled themselves out of the swamp and began their long journey to sobriety.

But they had their buttons pushed aplenty. Dr. Bob, treating alcoholics at St. Thomas Hospital, heard snide comments from other physicians who resented giving bed space to drunks. Bill W., struggling to launch a worldwide movement, took criticism from the very people he was helping. Almost every alcoholic, then and now, gets some heavy kidding from the world of drinkers.

What is the real problem in these instances? Are others pushing our buttons, or do we set ourselves up for this by being sensitive and vulnerable? Nobody could push our buttons if we didn't have buttons to push.

We no longer have to worry about button-pushers if we accept them as they are, realizing that we don't need their approval and can't really be hurt by anything they do or say. Our serenity in the face of such problems may actually serve to attract people to AA.

Nobody can push my buttons unless I let them. Today I'll be serene and calm no matter what others say and do. Thanks to the program, I'll not worry about certain individuals who try to get under my skin.

AVOIDING EMOTIONAL WHIRLPOOLS

Serenity If we were rafting down a rough river, we would try to steer away from whirlpools and rocky rapids. Living each day requires the same alertness.

We're asking for trouble if we drift into malicious discussions about other people—even those who seem to deserve it. We're also sliding into rocky rapids if we get into supercharged arguments about political and religious issues.

How do we avoid touchy situations that can lead to violent arguments or terrible breakdowns in personal relationships? We can begin by recognizing that we're not on this earth to judge, manipulate, or control other people. We'll do well today to keep our own performance up to a good standard.

We can also respond correctly to people who are misbehaving or whose opinions and beliefs seem hopelessly wrong. Borrowing an idea from one Twelve Step program, we can detach from such people with love, even if circumstances require continuing contact with them. At whatever cost, we must avoid emotional whirlpools and rocky rapids in life.

Looking ahead at the things that might happen today, I'll adjust my thinking for situations that could be troublesome or destructive. I will try especially hard to avoid trouble with my fellow workers.

THE GOOD THAT I DO

Action   Why do we hold back when we're offered the opportunity to help others or to do something unusually kind? Why is it that many people are reluctant to give of themselves unless rewarded with recognition or praise?

We may hold back because we do not understand that any good action always brings its own reward. Despite Shakespeare's timeless saying, the good we do is not "interred with our bones"—it does survive, now and in the future.

We've learned in Twelve Step programs that it's not really satisfying to work only for recognition and praise. There also has to be a confident feeling that our efforts are contributing to a large good with a worthwhile purpose. That's what makes AA so special to people who are completely devoted to it—we know that anything done for AA makes the world a better place.

We should also know that those who can help others are fortunate, well-favored people. Others may want to help, but lack the tools. We have the tools to give the help that changes lives—and the world.

The good that I do today is a treasure I'll always possess. I need not fear the act of letting my higher self take over and guide me.

FAKING IT, AND THEN MAKING IT

Finding the Spirit of the Thing We're sometimes advised to "fake it until you make it." But how can anything false really lead us to recovery? Aren't we told that this is an honest program?

We're not being dishonest by pushing ourselves to become actively involved in AA. The self-help movements have told us for years that we have to form an image of what we want to be in order to reach our goals. We are forming an image that corresponds to the sober people we want to be. We are actually rehearsing sober living and working to accept a picture of sobriety in our heart of hearts.

There's also much to be said for "faking it" enough to attend meetings and to try to benefit from association with people—even those we don't like. This puts us in line for the change we really need.

A lot of members say that they "white-knuckled it" during the first months or years of sobriety. If this worked to bring recovery, it had to be the right approach.

Even if there is rebellion within, today I'll talk and act like the sober person I want to be.

APRIL 23

WHEN AM I MANIPULATIVE?

Personal Relations   Without understanding our motives, we can easily lapse into behavior aimed at manipulating others. Sulking is a means of letting others know we are displeased and forcing them to attempt to win our approval. Flattery is a false expression of approval that we don't really feel—giving others good strokes for our own purpose. Withholding deserved praise is a means of putting others down, something we're likely to do because of our jealousy.

Manipulative behavior is almost always selfish behavior. It is usually a false means of trying to get our own way. It is certainly an immature way of dealing with people and situations.

The best way to avoid being manipulative is to be ourselves at all times. We have neither the right nor the responsibility to control or regulate other people. Our best approach, in trying to influence another's actions, is simply to state our own case with sincerity and honesty. Others must be free to act, free to choose, and free to make their own decisions without manipulative interference on our part.

I will be myself at all times today. I will not assume false roles simply for the purpose of bending others to my own will. Manipulative behavior is controlling behavior, which I must avoid.

DO I TRIGGER GOSSIP?

Personal Inventory   There is a saying that "listening to gossip is gossip." How true! If there were no listeners, there would never be any gossip.

Some of us who pride ourselves in refraining from gossip may still have a problem with it. It's possible we still keep open ears for any juicy gossip that could fall our way. We might also "shake the tree" if we believe another person has some gossip to share with us. This is done in seemingly innocent ways, sometimes just by mentioning the name of a person to another who may have strong opinions to express.

The harm of gossip lies in what we do to ourselves when we engage in it. There is no way we can continue to have spiritual growth if we practice gossip, even as passive listeners. Spiritual growth takes place within us, and it needs an environment completely free of any ill will.

Let's beware of any tendency to say things that induce others to gossip. At the same time, let's tune out gossip that seems to occur spontaneously. Gossip is the enemy of the growth we desire.

It is a real relief to know that today I have no desire to spread gossip or listen to it. This includes things I might read in magazines or newspapers.

FIXING NEEDS

Inventory AA pioneers once thought of their work as "fixing" drunks. That was dropped in AA, but "getting a fix" survives in the drug culture.

The truth is, we can't fix anybody, nor can we fix any problem with a destructive, mood-altering drug. What we're really seeking—what every compulsive person really seeks—is to fix the conflicting needs that tear us apart at the seams.

We can fix many of those needs over time if we practice Twelve Step principles. That "searching and fearless moral inventory," humbling though it may be, will expose the fierce drives that are consuming us. Sharing the truth about ourselves with others helps us understand both what is right and what is wrong in our lives. The power to change ourselves, when we desire it, comes from a Higher Power—God as we understand [God].

Somebody has summed this process up this way: "Need a fix? Fix the need!" We can use that idea to fix our needs today by following the Twelve Step program. At times, we may not even be completely aware of our real needs. This too will be revealed to us as we continue in the program.

I'll start my day by affirming that there's no need that can cause me to do anything destructive. As any problem arises, I learn how to fix my needs in healthy ways.

NEVER WITHHOLDING OURSELVES

Living Sober We may have let ourselves believe that we're supposed to display an attitude that expresses our opinions of others. If a person is crude and boorish, we should be cool and defensive for our self-protection. If a person is warm and friendly, we should respond in warm and friendly ways.

If we have believed these things, then we're actually letting others control our attitudes and behavior. We are letting personalities interfere with the high principles we are learning in AA. We are not living at the best possible level.

In reality, we should always display an attitude that reflects kindness, optimism, friendliness, and concern. The other person's disposition, whether it's sour or sweet, should have nothing to do with our being what we want to be. We should never withhold the fine inner qualities that develop and grow as we continue to live the program.

In time, we begin to learn that this attitude always comes back to us in the form of greater peace and happiness. And what's great about it is that it's always under our direct control!

As I go about my business today, I will express a kindliness and concern toward everybody. Nobody's behavior can make me adopt a suspicious or defensive attitude.

HAPPY PEOPLE ARE LIKEABLE

Personal Relations   Who are the people we really like, and like to be with? Most of the time, they are happy people, people who like themselves and others.

Being happy is almost the entire secret of being likable. Though no person can expect to be liked by everybody, the likable people have the inside track most of the time.

How do we become happy and thus likable? We're continuously told that happiness cannot be found in property, power, and prestige. It is rooted instead in self-acceptance, in feeling loved and wanted, and in giving genuine service, maybe just in the form of very useful work.

Twelve Step programs are structured to make us happy if we persevere long enough in working the individual steps. While it may seem contradictory, even people with heavy burdens and personal sorrows can find underlying happiness in the program. A great deal of this also hinges on our belief in a Higher Power and a confidence that we have a place in the universal system.

I can be happy today in spite of things that others would consider burdensome and depressing. Happiness really comes from God, and it also serves to attract friends into my life.

EXPECT MIRACLE-WORKING
COINCIDENCES

Spiritual Direction Somebody said that a wonderful coincidence is when God acts but does not choose to leave a signature. Wonderful coincidences are appearing every moment of the day. People who live the spiritual life are especially positioned to recognize and understand coincidences.

The founding of AA abounds with coincidences that boggle the mind. Almost by chance, the Oxford Group ideas found their way to Bill Wilson. A business trip took him to Akron where, coincidentally, an earnest group of Oxford Group people were trying to help Dr. Bob Smith to sobriety. With his business venture in collapse, Bill made the telephone call that put him in touch with Dr. Bob, eventually resulting in the launch of AA.

Such miraculous coincidences work for the fellowship, and they're also at work in our individual lives. If we look closely, we'll discover that many such coincidences helped bring about our recovery or some other blessing.

God is the guiding power behind these coincidences. What appears to be chance is really a marvelous intelligence coordinating random events for the good of all.

I'll have confidence today that God is always bringing positive results out of a number of random events.

REMEMBER THE PAST,
BUT DON'T LIVE IN IT

Living Today   In some ways, the Twelve Step recovery process invites trouble in dealing with the past. We're supposed to forget the past and live for today. But the opening thoughts delivered at meetings often review the past in painful detail, thus reinforcing the tendency to relive it. How should we approach this problem?

Our need is to remember the past while releasing any bitterness, regrets, or hurts connected with it. We must never *live* in the past, which we are doing when we feel either resentment or remorse about actions of ourselves or others. It is, however, helpful to *remember* what happened in the past so that we will no longer repeat the same mistakes.

We should also remember the past as a means of keeping ourselves both humble and honest. It should help us feel gratitude that we no longer have to live as we once did.

Remembering the past in open "lead" meetings is sometimes called "qualifying" as an alcoholic. It is an aid in carrying the message of recovery and a way of building more strength and understanding for today and tomorrow.

I'll be pleased today that I can remember the past without living in it. I am free from the old hurts and problems that would keep me from directing all of my energies and attention to what I am doing here and now.

APRIL 30

ADDICTED TO CRISIS

Personal Relations It's sometimes a surprise to learn that we mismanage our affairs even in sobriety. We may even find that we seem to be addicted to problem situations. It takes a crisis, it seems, to give us the energy and purpose we need to get things done.

One common form of this strange addiction is procrastination. Some of us have a tendency to put off important tasks until the very last moment, and then work overtime to get the job done.

Is this laziness? Maybe it is, to some extent. Maybe, however, we need an impending emergency to get motivated and energized to do what needs to be done. Maybe we're addicted to crisis.

If so, this may be another disease that can be arrested but not cured. We arrest it by slowly adopting better work habits and paying closer attention to schedules and deadlines. Working with greater efficiency, we'll have more time and energy for the things that really matter.

Today I don't need a crisis to take charge of my life and do what needs to be done. I'll tackle at least one thing I've been putting off, and either complete the task or get a good start on it.

May

MAY 1

ACCEPTING EQUAL TREATMENT

Growing Spiritually One of our AA friends was a district judge in a northern community. On his way to speak at our meeting, he was given a speeding ticket by a state policeman.

"Didn't you tell him you are a judge?" we wanted to know. Smiling sheepishly, he shook his head. It occurred to us, then, that acceptance of the speeding ticket without argument was also an exercise in principles for him. First, he was accepting the same laws he administered to others. Additionally, accepting the ticket was a working of the Tenth Step—". . . and when we were wrong promptly admitted it." Finally, he realized that the ticket may have been a disguised blessing to help him correct a tendency to speed.

As recovering alcoholics, we always function better when we accept such principles in our own lives. Every person is special, yet as part of the human race in general, we must accept the same treatment that is given to others. We can grow spiritually when we accept such equality without resentment or demands for special treatment.

As a human being, I know that today I'm subject to all the things that can happen to human beings. I will not demand or expect privileges that are not available on an equal basis to others.

MAY 2

LOOK OUT FOR POWER TRIPS

Understanding Hidden Motives   We can often use a lofty reason to disguise a hidden motive behind our actions. We might be seeking power over people's lives, for example, while claiming that "we're only out to help them." We may argue for a point of view only to establish a position of power. Such power trips are destructive, and others usually see them for what they really are.

If we've really accepted the principles of the Twelve Steps, we have no need for power trips. The logic of Step Eleven, for example, is that we'll always have the power needed to carry out what's in line with God's will for us. We do not have to jostle and manipulate others to establish our importance or our authority.

When we really come to terms with our own tendencies to take power trips, we'll be able to deal with others who come on strong with *their* power trips. We'll soon perceive that such threats usually fade when we refuse to resist them or be upset by them.

I'll undoubtedly meet people today who are maneuvering for power in different situations. I will neither criticize nor oppose them. My responsibility today is to avoid any of my own tendencies to take such power trips.

KNOWING A NEW FREEDOM

Spiritual Growth Most of us place a high value on freedom without always knowing what it really is, or ought to be. "Freedom" in the drinking world is often merely license to indulge ourselves without concern about consequences. This false freedom usually forces us into dependency or the need to rely on others to get us out of trouble.

The "new freedom" that comes out of the Twelve Steps is of a higher order. It means that by following principles in living we find choices and experiences that were never possible in the old life. We are free from the destructive behavior that always ended in pain and defeat.

This freedom is more of the spirit than of worldly things. It is knowing the truth about ourselves and life. As the Bible says, "You shall know the truth, and the truth shall make you free." In this new freedom, we no longer pursue activities that are ruinous and wasteful. We no longer deceive ourselves with painful illusions and false hopes, because we've learned to live and think on higher levels. Knowing the truth, we're free from alcohol and from the bad thinking that poisoned our lives and relationships.

Today I'll be grateful for the new freedom I have found in the program. I am free from the compulsions that caused me to hurt myself and others. I am free to choose new opportunities for service and self-expression.

SECRETS OF THE NEW HAPPINESS

Success in Living Most of us know whether other people are truly happy. What's odd, however, is that we don't often try to practice the things that bring happiness to others. Often, the happiness we're striving for is really a form of excitement—trying to be continuously stimulated so as not to be bored or depressed.

Excitement does not create happiness. We find true happiness when we learn to serve others in right ways; that is, without demanding their gratitude or some other recognition. We also find true happiness in self-acceptance—being generally satisfied with our lot in life and grateful for the self-improvement we've found. We find happiness, too, in keeping occupied with useful activities that place demands on our energies and abilities.

There is no such thing as a happy alcoholic who is still drinking. There are also recovering people who have not yet found happiness. But the program unlocks the secrets of happiness, and we do have members whose happiness is an example to others.

I can be happy one day at a time. I will make the choice to be happy today, and to let tomorrow come in its own time. Nothing can interfere with today's happiness.

TOUGH HONESTY?

Honesty The term *tough love* came into use to describe an attitude that aims to correct bad behavior by refusing to indulge or enable it. In the same way, we must recognize that there's such a thing as tough honesty when situations require us to deal with unpleasant facts.

One employer liked to compliment his subordinates even for work that he actually considered substandard. Later on, however, he would express his real opinions to an intermediate supervisor, who would then be forced to convey the bad news to the workers involved. The employer thought he was being kind, when he was actually being deceptive and treacherous simply because he wanted to be liked.

We have a moral obligation to practice tough honesty whenever it is required. If something unacceptable needs to be dealt with, we must do so in a timely manner—taking care to be as reasonable and fair as possible in stating our case. (We should not, of course, use this honesty as an opportunity to be cruel or vindictive.)

Being honest in this way with others is also a reminder that we should always be honest with ourselves.

Today I'll face the need for real honesty whenever it's required. I'll be up front with myself and others about anything that must be faced and dealt with. I will not use supposed kindness as an excuse for bearing false witness.

DEALING WITH FEAR

Challenges Some of us suffer from a free-floating anxiety that is like a general fear, while others have specific fears that cause distress. Sometimes the specific fears are easier to face, because they can at least be identified. Most of us dread the other kind—a sort of general apprehension that things are not well or that something very bad is about to happen.

It's reasonable to have some fear when facing trouble or risk. It's unreasonable, however, to let fear keep us from acting in our own best interests. A review of the past may show that many of us did that while drinking—and brought even more calamities upon ourselves.

Whatever the fear, the answer is always the same. We must apply our principles to the problem, take any reasonable action, and then place the outcome in God's hands. No person can do more than this.

This will not bring permanent victory over fear. It will, however, give us confidence in the program as a tool for dealing with fears that arise in the future.

I may have to deal with fear today, but I will accept it as part of the human condition. I know that I have great spiritual resources to deal with any fear that might arise, and this gives me confidence and reassurance.

DID I HAVE A DYSFUNCTIONAL FAMILY?

Healing the Past We hear much about the long-term effects of growing up in a dysfunctional family. Many alcoholics, in fact, have bitter memories of their own parents' drinking, and may feel this caused needless deprivation and misery.

Whether our families were dysfunctional or not, we must agree that most of our parents did the best they could. We cannot bring back the past—nor can they—and it is best released, forgiven, and forgotten. Our wisest course is to use the tools of the program to reach the maturity and well-being that will bring happiness into our own lives. This will not happen, however, if we believe that growing up in a dysfunctional home has left us permanently impaired.

In our fellowship, we can find endless examples of people who used the Twelve Steps to overcome all kinds of emotional and physical disabilities. Just when we start thinking something in our past is a permanent handicap, we meet other people who survived the same bitter experiences and are living life to the fullest. They've cleared away the wreckage of their past in order to build wisely for the future.

I'll remember today that I am not bound or limited by anything that was ever done or said to me. I face the day with self-confidence and a sense of expectancy, knowing that I am really a fortunate person with many reasons to be grateful.

REGRETS OVER ROADS NOT TAKEN

Releasing the Past   Looking back, every one of us can point to moments when we made choices that helped set the course of our lives. It's easy to waste time and energy wondering what our lives would have been like if other choices had been made at these critical points.

Such thinking is mostly a waste of time and may reflect dissatisfaction with our lives today. Whatever our past mistakes, the decisions we made that brought us sobriety were the correct ones. Realizing this, many of us even come to feel gratitude for the problem that brought us into the program.

We are never able to say with certainty that different choices made earlier in life would have been better in the long run. Bill W., an AA cofounder, said that a business setback moved him to make the calls that led him to Dr. Bob, the other cofounder. Had his business venture succeeded, it's doubtful that Bill would have been thinking about helping another alcoholic.

The best choice any of us can make is to turn such matters and questions over to our Higher Power. We have a duty to do the best we can with today's opportunities and conditions.

I'll live today in the present. The good experiences from the past are always with me, and I can benefit from any lessons learned by my mistakes.

THE IMPORTANCE OF HOPE

Maintaining Optimism As a great virtue, hope is ranked with faith and love. But those of us caught in the thicket of alcoholism and other addictions had much experience with hopes that turned out to be merely cruel illusions. In recovery, however, hope has a sound purpose. It is really a form of optimism, an underlying belief that things will work out in spite of the obstacles and problems we face. This helps provide the strength and energy we need to succeed in the face of opposition and setbacks.

We also owe much of our recovery to the capacity for hope that was in our friends and family members. Henrietta D., the wife of AA Member Number Three, told an interviewer that she had never lost hope that her husband would eventually recover. She saw it as the answer to her hope and prayers when Bill W. and Dr. Bob arrived at her husband's bedside in Akron's City Hospital—and when he left, he never drank again.

Hope is the optimism that keeps us moving toward our highest good. Let's keep it alive.

I'll face my day with the underlying belief that things will work out in the long run. I'll refuse to be overwhelmed by temporary setbacks.

DOING THE IMPOSSIBLE THINGS

Achievements   One of our friends became critical of our AA group, suggesting that we were limiting ourselves by focusing solely on recovery when so many other accomplishments waited on the horizon. After all, isn't it written that "with God, all things are possible"?

It is indeed true that we should place no limits at all on our Higher Power. Even nonbelievers will admit that nature and the universe show power and intelligence that are far beyond our understanding.

What limits us is our own ability to receive and use our Higher Power in proper ways. Even if our journey in the program gives us boundless self-confidence, we must always deal with our own selfish tendencies and the temptation to seek personal gain rather than personal improvement. Certain kinds of success can be fully as toxic as any drug. Some of us, in fact, can deal with disappointments more effectively than we can with too much success.

The idea of "doing impossible things" is fully covered in the Steps. We seek knowledge of "God's will for us and the power to carry that out." This means that we'll find the wherewithal to do anything that belongs in our lives. Anything else is needless and perhaps even dangerous.

I'll not feel that I lack faith simply because I haven't been able to reach certain goals. My Higher Power will show me how to balance my life so I can accept what is rightfully mine. There is no need to do the seemingly "impossible" unless it is in the order of things.

MAY 11

UNFAIR PEOPLE

Personal Relations   Now and then, we encounter people who are almost blatant in their unfairness to others. We may make a 200-mile drive to a customer who is completely unprepared to see us, despite having had advanced notice. Or we may have a friend who is openly critical of our shortcomings while completely overlooking his or her own.

Unfair though these people may be, they give us the opportunity to exercise spiritual muscles. We can improve ourselves and the world by refusing to retaliate when such unfairness occurs.

The long-term benefit is that many of these unfair people change or fade out of our lives. As we handle such things spiritually, we recall times when we too were unfair, and we realize that such faults are part of the human condition. We are lucky people because we're being given the opportunity to raise the human condition to a higher level. We also hear that "life isn't fair, it's just there!" Not understanding life completely, we're not sure about its fairness. What we are sure about is that we value fairness and can show more of it now that we're sober.

I will not seek out unfair treatment today, but neither will I be upset if it occurs. If it does, I'll deal with it as another lesson in my spiritual growth.

REPEATING THE OLD HURTS

Serenity It's been pointed out that the real meaning of *resentment* is to "re-feel" an old injury. This means that we let ourselves feel again the pain we had when we were previously wronged.

Common sense tells us that this is a foolish practice. But with emotions like resentment, common sense can be crowded out. It is a rare person who can avoid resentment about matters that caused deep injury. Resentment is so much a part of everyday life, in fact, that it's considered abnormal not to resent a real wrong.

We've also been conditioned to believe that we're being spineless and wimpy if we don't become outraged by certain injustices and wrongs. There's a difference, however, between feeling strongly that something is wrong and being sullen and resentful about it. The first kind of feeling helps us remedy the problem; the second feeling simply intensifies our hurt. Under no circumstances can we afford resentment.

I'll make this day resentment-free, despite the currents of feeling and bitterness around me. "Re-feeling" old injuries is not the way to the happier life I seek.

WHO'S TO BLAME?

Personal Responsibility Unless we're unusual, we've probably accepted the widespread practice of blaming certain individuals and groups when trouble occurs. Most likely, we'll also have people whom we blame for our own difficulties: unloving parents, careless teachers, unfair bosses, and others on an endless list.

However accurate it may be, such blame-placing does nothing constructive. It really serves only to reinforce our bitterness and resentment, thus assuring that more of the same "injustices" will come to us.

The real truth is that we have no complete explanation for the world's individual and social wrongs. While certain individuals are admittedly guilty of wrongdoing, it often turns out that they've also been victims of cruelty or neglect. Our goal, as people committed to a spiritual way of life, is to rise above all blame placing while striving for improvement in our own treatment of others.

Though I may read and hear much to the contrary, I'll resist the notion that certain people or groups must be held accountable for the world's problems. I'll focus my attention, this day, on improvement in my own life.

MAKING LAWS FOR OURSELVES

Attaining Freedom   Being human means that we're subject to all the laws and limitations that apply to human beings. We should not, however, put more limitations on ourselves than might be required by our situation.

Recovering people should be able to do anything within their capabilities. It's usually a mistake to think that our problem means forfeiture of opportunities. One person, for example, often told his friends that he could not return to his former profession in sales because "nobody wants to hire an alcoholic salesman."

But it is not written anywhere that firms will not gladly welcome a capable sales associate who is recovering. Many alcoholics do return to their former employment upon recovery. Our friend was simply making a law for himself by believing he was blocked from this field.

Let's always remember that recovery is freedom, not bondage. And let's see ourselves doing anything that's reasonable and proper for others.

Having rejoined the human race, I'll enthusiastically accept all the advantages and opportunities others have.

MAY 15

TRUSTING OTHERS

Personal Relationships   Some people trust others too much, while a few seem to have no trust at all. Either stance is wrong and leads to some kind of trouble.

As we grow in our Twelve Step program, we learn the truth about trust. We can trust others if our expectations aren't too high. We have to remember, however, that as human beings they can fail us. However, it's also unrealistic to be suspicious of everyone. The truth is that most people aren't out to get us or to hurt us. They are pursuing their own interests, just as we must do.

As we grow emotionally, we come to see that we have less difficulty trusting others. We no longer make outrageous demands on them or stretch their patience to the limits. We also realize that there are many times when we can work cooperatively with everybody's interests in mind.

I'll think realistically about others today, being careful not to expect either too much or too little from them. I'll certainly not expect more from them than I could reasonably expect from myself.

TREES DON'T GROW TO THE SKY

Progress Release from a compulsion can be a dramatic experience. It may also mean immediate release from vexing problems caused by the compulsion. This time can bring such a sense of well-being that it's sometimes called the "honeymoon" or "Cloud Nine" period.

In any growth process, however, we must remember that a law of diminishing returns sets in. This is expressed in the saying that trees don't grow to the sky. At some point, we will discover that our joyous feeling of pleasure has cooled down to an ordinary state of feeling well, that we are not becoming increasingly joyous by the day.

There's nothing wrong with such a mental plateau. If we're practicing the Twelve Step program, we're still moving forward, onward, and upward. Diminishing returns must still be counted as returns.

I'll accept today's progress with gratitude and humility. I won't expect more than a reasonable feeling of well-being and contentment, but that is considerable.

REHEARSING OUTCOMES

Serenity Imagination is undeniably a human faculty that accounts for much progress. Compulsive people, however, can use imagination in a most destructive way.

One destructive practice is that of rehearsing in our minds the outcome of some threat or problem, usually expecting the worst. While we should not avoid facing real problems, it's wrong to assume that the worst will always happen. This tendency to anticipate the worst possible outcome can actually produce the very outcome we'd like to avoid, thus making it a self-fulfilling prophecy.

We can deal with such pessimistic thinking by reminding ourselves that God is in charge and will bring our good to pass in just the right way. If we're going to rehearse anything, let it be an outcome that includes the best for everybody, including ourselves.

I'll expect the best today, knowing that all outcomes and results are in God's hands.

NO LIMITS ON OUR HIGHER POWER

The Spiritual Way One ancient saying claims that "with God, all things are possible." That's quite a statement, one we may claim to believe without living as though we do.

What it really means is that God exists outside the conditions and restrictions that make our own lives so limited. The more we can move into conscious contact with God, the more freedom and power we will experience.

It might be said that all real human progress is of the same order. Every advancement in science really reveals more information about God and the universe. We are always discovering new possibilities for humankind as we stretch the frontiers of knowledge.

Our most serious lag is in learning to understand ourselves and each other. It is humbling to realize that the ideas we're using in Twelve Step programs have been around for centuries. Faced with impossible problems, we must remember that God can solve these problems if only we ask.

I'll follow today the old idea of working as if everything depended on me and believing as if everything depended on God.

PRINCIPLES ARE ENDURING

Problem Solving We often emphasize "principles before personalities" in Twelve Step programs, sometimes without fully understanding what's involved. The real message of this slogan is that we should treat people equally while following certain guidelines in our own actions.

While we are influenced by strong personalities, we cannot rely on them for complete guidance and direction. People can betray us or simply fail us through no fault of their own. Principles, on the other hand, are enduring and will be with us long after personal relationships wither away.

One unfailing principle for living is to live each day remembering that God is guiding and directing all actions and outcomes. While we will be grateful for the assistance and cooperation of others, we will not hold them responsible for our successes or failures.

I'll live today with the belief that God's good plan is working in all people's lives. I will not expect too much or too little of others, but rather will deal with them fairly and decently.

GRATITUDE IS NOT NATURAL

Gratitude "Nobody ever gave me a helping hand," a young alcoholic complained, having landed in prison. "My life has been one bad break after another."

While this person indeed had bad breaks, it's doubtful that he'd never been given a helping hand by somebody. If we have no gratitude, it's likely that we don't ever recognize a helping hand when it is extended. We may have believed any assistance we took was our right, even resenting our benefactors.

The remedy for such immature thinking is a conscious effort to cultivate gratitude. If we're not aware of feeling it, we can at least act as if we have it. Thank people for any favor, no matter how small. Express appreciation for the wonderful people around you. Give people praise at every opportunity.

This will help start a current of gratitude that can be amplified in time. You'll come to recognize many helping hands.

Today I'll be grateful and appreciative of everything in my life. I'll let gratitude build up in my life until I can feel it and others can sense that I have it.

WHAT IS A DISAPPOINTMENT?

Handling My Outlook   Try as we will for success and achievement, we still must face a number of disappointments in our lives. We may be disappointed by a sales presentation that failed, a repair project that became a nightmare, or a vacation plan that turned sour. How can we handle such disappointments in the spirit of the Twelve Step program?

We must remember not to be too hard on ourselves when disappointments occur. Disappointments are part of the human experience, not misfortunes that come only to certain individuals. If we've done our best in any situation, we are not responsible if it did not work out.

Even more important, we should use every disappointment as a learning experience. It's always possible that one disappointment will provide kernels of truth that will help us succeed in our next effort. Many people point to specific disappointments or setbacks as times when they were able to find new direction.

There are even times when disappointment in a lesser enterprise clears the way for success in a larger one. Whatever the outcome, no disappointment need be final—nor should we take it as proof that we're somehow inadequate and unworthy.

I will be positive in my outlook, expecting every effort to be effective and successful. If disappointment comes, however, I will take it in stride, knowing that it's only a temporary detour in my successful life.

EMOTIONAL SOBRIETY MAY BE ELUSIVE

Serenity It is easy to know when one is maintaining sobriety as far as alcohol is concerned. Emotional sobriety is more difficult to measure, because it is usually gauged by our behavior and feelings in response to people and situations.

If we lack emotional sobriety, we are likely to end up in "dry drunks." This means we lose emotional control under pressure or when threatened. We may think we have this control, yet find ourselves falling apart when seemingly small problems come up.

Maybe we have to accept that we will never have all the emotional control that we admire in others. This emotional sensitivity may even be part of our alcoholism. Most important, we must ensure that emotional binges do not become binges involving real booze.

Nor should we judge ourselves too harshly when we undergo another emotional binge, or "dry drunk." Such judgmental attitudes, even toward ourselves, may be a form of false pride.

Today I'll seek all the serenity I can find. If I lose my cool temporarily, I'll accept it as part of my general problem and get back to orderly thinking as quickly as possible.

AVOID THE PARALYSIS OF ANALYSIS

Practical Spirituality The good news of the Twelve Step program is that we have a Higher Power whose presence serves as a source of guidance and understanding as we go through each day. Letting this Power work through us is only a matter of will—God draws as near to us as we wish to draw near to God.

As we let our Higher Power work, we remember that no scientific explanation for this process is necessary. We could paralyze our spiritual activity by trying to analyze it, thus bringing about an undesirable "paralysis of analysis." It's also not necessary to win another's endorsement of what we're trying to do. We must not be influenced by any scorn or ridicule of our efforts.

All that's necessary is that we know God in our own lives and stay faithful to our program. We let the presence of God work freely and smoothly as we go about our business.

I'll work today with the comfortable knowledge that God is really doing work through me.

GUIDANCE AND POWER
IN MAKING DECISIONS

Higher Power The Twelve Step movement grew out of an earlier society that emphasized taking "quiet times" and seeking continuous guidance in a group setting. While this isn't usually practiced by Twelve Step groups anymore, such exercises are still recommended for individuals.

Our needs in seeking guidance are twofold: First, we must reach a belief that our Higher Power is always available to supply the guidance and power we need. Second, we must take care to set aside personal opinions and prejudices while letting real guidance come through. We can easily fall into serious error by assuming that our own impulses and prejudices are "the will of God" for ourselves and others.

How can we identify real guidance when it comes? Usually, we have a sense of peace and rightness about a God-inspired decision. This will be accompanied by a confidence that the correct way will be shown to us, perhaps a step at a time. The right decision will also be morally correct, involving no harm to others.

I'll seek the guidance of my Higher Power in all things today, knowing that I have within myself the capacity to heed such guidance and follow it.

FORGETTING PAST FAILURES

Living Today "You never do anything right!" Some of us carry this accusation deep in our minds, perhaps from childhood. We remember past mistakes and failures, sometimes dredging them up again when new failures occur.

When we do this, we unduly burden ourselves with a past that should be released and forgotten. The result of past mistakes was a feeling of inadequacy and helplessness that prolonged our sickness. In those troubled days, we were trying to solve our problems in ways that actually made the problems worse. On that path, there was no hope of a real solution.

Today our failure and mistakes are but signs that we are still human and still fall short of perfection. But now we can use failure to good advantage and even learn from it. Our best progress will come when we separate ourselves from the mistakes and failures of the past.

Today I will not believe that "I never did anything right." I will go through the day knowing that I am capable and effective, and have the help of my Higher Power in everything I do.

TODAY'S PROBLEM

Orderly Living   Facing a vexing or even threatening problem, we sometimes feel a sense of hopelessness or futility. "How will I ever get through this situation?" we think.

The truth is we have probably worked our way through many situations much like today's problem. It is a wonder, for example, that most of us survived the crises brought on by our compulsion. We will certainly be able to work through or around today's problem.

The Twelve Step program is a plan for mastering the problems of life. As we apply its principles in all of our affairs, we find improvements beginning to appear. We also can find the confidence and fortitude that we've always needed.

Knowing that my Higher Power is in the midst of the situation, I'll face today's problem with the assurance of an outcome that will be for my highest good.

MAY 27

WHO IS IMPORTANT?

Respect for People The Twelve Step movement grew out of an earlier society, the Oxford Group, whose members believed in "key people." They embraced the idea that attracting promising individuals with high standing would, in turn, attract others.

We've also had such people in AA and other Twelve Step groups, and we are grateful for their examples and efforts. We've learned, however, not to view one person as more important than another. We could even harm a recovering person by focusing on his or her personal prestige in the community. Our purpose is to help people get well, not to run a club emphasizing social standing.

We'll find our program working much better if we treat all people equally, and view them as equal in the sight of God. We have a standing in God's sight that is eternal and everlasting.

I'll extend kind and generous thoughts toward every person I meet today. We are all children of equal standing in the sight of God.

EVERYDAY RISKS

Courage We have to take certain risks if we hope to achieve anything. Applying for a job entails a risk of rejection. Saving money carries a risk of losing it. Falling in love can result in heartbreak.

We have to take such risks because life is ordered that way. We are here to learn, and learning includes pressing into unknown situations where we could fail.

God could have created us in such a way that we could either avoid risks or not be unduly concerned about them. Animals, for example, live with risks but do not seem to worry about them.

We must accept risk as part of God's plan for us. We also are given tools for working with uncertainties. We have our innate intelligence and a capacity for prudent, reasoned action. We have friends who will help us. Above all, we have our Higher Power, who guides and directs us through all sorts of risky conditions.

I cannot face life without also facing uncertainties. Today I'll accept risk as a part of ordinary living.

GUARDING AGAINST
DISGUISED HOSTILITY

Fairness One of the pitfalls in continued recovery is a tendency to become self-righteous and judgmental. Sometimes this fuses into a hostility directed toward newcomers or chronic "slippers." Now and then, we've seen grumpy older members demanding that those who slip get honest.

While we may be right in concluding that a person is not showing honesty, we have no right to denounce or expose anyone in a group setting. Far from helping the person, we may be showing off. If there is hostility in our words or manner, the other person will certainly sense it.

The best group setting for good recovery is always one that expresses warmth, acceptance, and understanding. There are few, if any, times when a verbal assault can be justified. Before we lash out at another person's lack of honesty, we must take an honest look at our own motives and feelings.

I'll face the day with a feeling of goodwill and acceptance in my dealings with every person I meet. If I attend a meeting, I'll show the same warmth and acceptance toward every person there.

CIVILIANS WHO SHOW RESENTMENT

Healthy Thinking As compulsive people, we're urged to watch resentments carefully. These negative feelings can flare up out of nowhere and bring terrible destruction.

This sensitivity in spotting our own resentments also makes us more aware of resentments in others—perhaps people who are not alcoholic and thus are considered "normal."

When this happens, we have no responsibility to point their resentment out to them. Our best approach is to deal with them as cordially as possible and to withdraw gracefully if their resentment is directed at us. This teaches us that resentment is a universal human problem—not just an affliction of alcoholics and other compulsive people.

While guarding against resentment in myself today, I'll not be surprised or hurt when it appears in others. If it does, I will not feel hurt or surprised, knowing that it's a human problem.

ARE SOBRIETY DATES IMPORTANT?

Practical Thinking Observing anniversaries of getting sober has become a time-honored custom in AA. Many group name lists include the individual members' sobriety dates. It's also customary in many groups to celebrate anniversaries with cakes and to award coins with numerals denoting years of sobriety.

To outsiders, this custom may seem frivolous. What is the benefit in celebrating the day one took the last drink or in adding up the number of sober years?

These celebrations of sobriety dates actually underscore the important goal of staying *continuously sober*. We may know alcoholics who "went back out" from time to time, and then failed to come back at all. Members who slip and do come back tell us that it was an agonizing experience, and that they feared they wouldn't have another chance to lead a sober life. We also hear people say: "I may have another drunk in me, but I'm not sure I can find another sobering up."

The message is clear: Get sober, mark that date, and continue to build on it. We stress the importance of sobriety when we acknowledge the importance of sobriety dates.

I'll stay sober today. Whatever my length of sobriety, I want to honor it and build on it.

June

JUNE 1

SELFISH IS ALWAYS WRONG

Inventory It's unfortunate that members sometimes refer to the Twelve Step idea as a "selfish" program. If selfishness is considered a human shortcoming, why should we describe our wonderful program as selfish?

What we're really trying to say, it seems, is that our true self-interest lies in the direction of helping others and sharing our experience and strength with them. To do this is to lose the "bondage of self" that is so destructive in the life of every compulsive person.

In this process, we'll probably also discover that too much self-concern has made us unhappy and ill. Selfish, we're likely to learn, is always bad.

When people say that ours is a selfish program, they really intend to convey the idea that it's a "self-improvement" program. It's our concern about others that leads to the higher forms of self-improvement.

Though exercising prudence and good judgment, I'll take a healthy interest in helping others and sharing with them today. I know that my Higher Power will be with me in all of my actions.

WHY ADMITTING WE'RE WRONG IS RIGHT

Right Action Sometimes it's painful or almost impossible to admit that we've been wrong. This means we'll probably go on making the same mistakes until we're finally forced to face the truth. Why does this happen?

The problem lies with what we call the ego in our Twelve Step discussions. We commit ourselves to defending this ego at all times, especially around people who seem to put us down. Far from being a minor correction, any admission of wrong feels like total defeat, at least in our warped way of looking at things.

We can release ourselves from this bondage simply by coming to see that admitting and facing our wrongs is essential to growth. A store manager who overstocks a certain item "admits" the mistake by putting the goods on a clearance sale and getting rid of them. We can cut any loss in the same way by admitting a mistake and going on to a better course of action.

I'll not plan to make any mistakes today, but I'll hold myself in readiness to admit them if they occur. This is no threat to my ego. I am much more than my mistakes.

JUNE 3

SELF-HELP OR MUTUAL AID?

Assisting Others The Twelve Step movement is sometimes called a self-help program. This falls short of describing what it really is. *Mutual aid* might be a better term.

Self-help implies that an individual will help himself or herself. Mutual aid is a much different sort of thing. With mutual aid, we do help ourselves, but we have found that the best way to do this is by helping each other. Self-help says, "I can do it," whereas mutual aid says, "We can do it."

We should not dismiss the idea of self-help or of doing one's best in achieving self-improvement. We must know, however, that we need the assistance and loving help of others for our highest growth. There are times when we will feel helpless and alone. That's when mutual aid will carry the day for us and perhaps even save our lives.

I'll realize today that I have a bond with others, and that I can achieve my highest good only in mutual service with them.

JUNE 4

NEEDING TO RECEIVE CREDIT

Humility "Is it wrong to want credit for the good things I do?" a person asked at a Twelve Step meeting. "Why do people say my ego is showing just because I feel I should get proper credit?"

We should, indeed, receive the right amount of praise and recognition for the good things we do. We have to remember, however, that we're trying to get this from human beings—many of whom are poorly informed or indifferent. Whatever credit we receive will be influenced by others' perceptions. Sometimes we will be praised too lavishly; at other times, insufficiently.

But the real question is not whether others give us the right amount of praise or credit. The question we should really ask is *why* we need such recognition. If we are doing a good thing or have made progress, isn't that sufficient reward? What can receiving credit do for us that we do not already have?

I'll take as my guide today the belief that right action is its own reward. I do not need credit or recognition from others, although I'll appreciate it if it comes.

JUNE 5

LOOKING AT THE LONG TERM

Living Today Though we're encouraged to live one day at a time, we must also be aware of the future. We should not knowingly do anything today that creates unneeded risks and penalties further down the road.

We should not, for example, take on unreasonable debt simply to live well today. We should not put off things that will get worse with time. We should not avoid unpleasant decisions that will have to be made sooner or later.

Living one day at a time really means planning to do our best each day. While we cannot predict or control the future, we do have a responsibility to act so that our tomorrows will also be good days for living.

I'll face today with the confidence that all my actions will be good for the long term as well as for today.

JUNE 6

MY OPPORTUNITIES ARE IN CHANGE

Personal Growth   It's common to hear a recovering person voice apprehension about an impending change. This apprehension only results from our fear that change will mean loss.

There can never be any permanent loss if we are solidly anchored in our spiritual program. Our Higher Power is the guiding force in all change and will make all things right as events unfold.

We should also remember that change brought us to our present situation. Any good we now enjoy came to us by a certain process. Even painful experiences have been valuable lessons.

There is no way we can avoid change; it is a built-in condition of life. We can accept it more gracefully if we view it as God's way of bringing us opportunity.

Any change that I sense today is but a signal for the arrival of new opportunities. Even if changes seem uncomfortable, I'll welcome all such change.

DECIDING OUTCOMES

Guidance No matter how limited our opportunities may be, we always have choices and decisions to make. With any choice or decision, it's only good sense to make the one that seems likely to have the best outcome.

If we're following our program, however, we should not be dismayed when outcomes turn out to be unfavorable or take turns that disappoint us. We can see only dimly into the future, and we have no way of knowing what will eventually come about as a result of our choices.

We do know that the meeting of the first two AA members actually came about as a result of a business disappointment. We can always find other examples of disappointing outcomes that proved to be good breaks as time passed.

This is not an attempt to rationalize bad situations. If God is in charge of our lives, we need not fear what each outcome might be.

Though I will choose and decide as sensibly as possible, I'll not be excessively concerned about outcomes. My long-term good is assured as I follow God's plan in my life. "For those who love God, all things work together for good."

JUNE 8

QUALITY OF SOBRIETY

Self-Improvement There is such a thing as length—or quantity—of sobriety, and there is also quality. It's generally accepted that sobriety ought to be something more than the single process of staying free from alcohol or drugs.

We're on shaky ground, however, when we begin passing judgment on another person's quality of sobriety. We only have responsibility for the quality of our own sobriety, and it is not for us to decide how another should think or live.

We may not be able to avoid noticing others' actions that we consider to be wrong, but we can keep our thoughts and opinions to ourselves. If we do wish to voice any opinions, it should be in terms of our own inventory—not the other person's.

Some old-timers in Twelve Step programs develop a crankiness that borders on resentment. Out of this crankiness come complaints about the way newcomers work the program. Our only responsibility is to treat these complaints with good humor and to avoid becoming cranky ourselves. Recovering alcoholics must continue to have the freedom to select any quality of sobriety they choose.

Today I'll strive for a high-quality sobriety that includes cheerfulness, confidence, patience, and good humor. I won't be responsible for monitoring another's sobriety.

JUNE 9

DO I FEEL UNEASY?

Serenity   When facing difficult situations, we can expect to feel a certain amount of discomfort. What's more often a problem for compulsive people is being tense and apprehensive even when things seem to be going well.

Although many explanations are offered for this unpleasant feeling, the solution is to be found in the Twelve Steps. The more secure we feel in our program, the less apprehension we'll have in facing the problems of living. With the program as our foundation, we will continue to develop more self-assurance as we go along.

We may not immediately find this self-assurance, yet we should not hold back from normal duties and responsibilities. Most of the world's work and accomplishments are undertaken by people who do not necessarily feel confident and self-assured all the time. Why should it be any different for us?

Whether I feel confident or not, I'll do my best today. I know that my fellowship, my program, and my Higher Power are fully supporting me.

EXPECTING QUICK RESULTS

Acceptance Most human progress comes slowly, though we see exciting breakthroughs at various times. The same is true in the lives of individuals. Though a few people do make exciting leaps forward, most of us must be content with gradual, steady improvements.

Our problem as compulsive people is in wanting quick results *all the time.* In fact, one of the things that reinforced our addiction was the continuous need for a quick fix. We saw life as something that should be taken in frantic gulps. When a sudden break or advantage appeared, it never really satisfied us. There was always the hunger for more.

We can find real satisfaction, however, in accepting progress in small stages. If we are having small gains here and there, we are on the road to improvement. A surprising amount can be accomplished when we are moving continuously ahead, one small step at a time.

The old fable of the tortoise and the hare still applies in human affairs. If we continue to move ahead, even at a slow speed, we will reach our goals.

I'll be content today with whatever progress I can make. If I'm expecting too many quick results, I might be setting myself up for disappointment.

JUNE 11

WHAT CAN WE CHANGE?

Handling Limitations There's always danger that resignation will masquerade as acceptance. In Twelve Step programs, we must learn the difference between the two. Resignation refers to putting up with conditions that we should actually change; it regards self-imposed limitation. Acceptance means recognizing reality and becoming comfortable with it.

We might resign ourselves to bad treatment that is unacceptable, or we might put up with personal shortcomings that we could change. When someone points this out, we defend ourselves by asserting that we're practicing acceptance.

As human beings and children of God, we are entitled to live with dignity and to receive fair treatment. We should never resign ourselves to anything that robs us of this basic humanity. Our Higher Power will show us how to eliminate resignation if we have been practicing it. The message of the program is that we never have to *accept* the things we can and should change.

Today if I am uncomfortable with something, I'll ask myself if I've been practicing resignation instead of acceptance. There may be many things in my life that can and should be changed.

BEING RIGHT OR WRONG

Honesty   Step Ten advises us to promptly admit it when we're wrong. Perhaps there should be another Step warning us not to be too confident when we're sure we're right.

It's true that there are many times when we are right. It's also possible, however, that we might be only 99 percent right, and that tiny fraction of error could mean our downfall.

Something is also wrong when we find ourselves vigorously asserting that we're right. We don't have to "admit it" when we're right because being right speaks for itself. In the long run, truth and right action don't really have to be defended. Part of being right is the willingness to believe that we may be wrong, however hard that is to accept.

If I'm wrong today, I'll admit it. If I'm right, I'll refrain from announcing it with too much assurance.

JUNE 13

PROGRESS IN STAGES

A Day at a Time The world of addictions is not known for encouraging personal qualities such as patience. It's more of a world where people dream of world-shaking achievement that will set everything right in an instant and put us on Easy Street forever.

This false world was really one in which we were seeking excitement and quick victories. We simply didn't realize that happiness could be found in the patient, persistent, everyday work that most people perform.

Living sensibly, we can easily see ourselves making progress as we complete the ordinary tasks of living. There can be accomplishment in doing the little things, and there can be enjoyment in activities that once seemed boring and dull. Great pleasure and peace can come from simply taking time to "smell the roses."

I'll remember that the excitement and pleasure I need are to be found in the place where I am now, and I can get the best out of it.

JUNE 14

TRUE SATISFACTION

Contentment True satisfaction never comes from feeding addiction. Nothing is ever enough. The only possible outcomes for those who do not seek recovery from their addictions will be complete breakdown and untimely death.

St. Augustine explained why it's impossible for humans to find true satisfaction in pursuing pleasure. "Thou hast made us for thyself and our hearts are restless until they repose in thee," he wrote, with reference to the Divine.

As we come to understand that true satisfaction comes from the Spirit, we will, surprisingly, receive more satisfaction from the worldly things we use. We will begin to look upon our possessions for the service they give rather than as things that should make us happy. A new car should give us comfortable, satisfactory transportation, but it cannot give us peace and true self-esteem. New clothes can please us, but they will not do anything for our spiritual depression.

Why didn't we know this all along? Probably because we falsely believed that certain possessions would bring fulfillment. They can't do that, but when we are thinking right, our appreciation of everything should increase.

I'll not expect true satisfaction in this world, although I'll get more out of it if I put things in right order.

WHAT IS AN ADDICTIVE DISEASE?

Facing Facts   Now that Twelve Step programs address a multitude of compulsions, arguments flare up about whether these should be called "addictions" or "diseases."

For the person with the problem, it's not important what terms the professional community wants to apply to the affliction. The most useful function of such terms has been to help people understand the seriousness of their situation. The disease concept of alcoholism, for example, took the focus off sin and weak willpower while supplying good reasons the alcoholic should never attempt to drink again.

All that we need to know about any compulsive malady is that we're drawn into it by certain "triggering" actions. Whether it's called a disease or an addiction, it is certainly a fatal condition if not arrested.

I'll keep the facts straight today about my problem area. Whatever it's called, it must not be allowed to destroy my life.

SOLVING OUR COMMON PROBLEM

Recovery Twelve Step programs bring together people who admit certain behaviors that society often views with pity or contempt. Some of these behaviors, such as alcoholism and gambling, are heavily stigmatized.

Though we often talk about "our common problem," the thing we have most in common with each other is that we're human beings who share the human condition. No one is really immune from the similar problems that beset us.

That's why somebody once remarked, only in half-jest, that "alcoholics are like normal people, only more so." We have to remember that the people around us are no different from us in that they are subject to such feelings as pride, resentment, self-pity, and discouragement.

Our common problem is really that we're human beings who need a spiritual life in order to become our true selves. This can turn a problem into a new life if we accept the program.

Today I'll look upon all people with understanding and acceptance. Everyone shares the same feelings that drive me, and everyone deserves my warmth and understanding.

IS THE GOLDEN RULE APPLICABLE?

Inventory Some people say the Golden Rule is impractical or believe it can work only if everybody begins following it at the same time.

We learn in Twelve Step programs that the Golden Rule *does* work. We start by taking our own inventory, whether or not others do. We make amends for our own wrongs, even when amends are not made to us. We think rightly about others, no matter how they think about us.

From time to time, we also receive a cosmic hint that the Golden Rule is far more than a mere human ideal expressed in an ancient time. It really appears to be one way of stating a law of life. We should treat others as we want to be treated because, in time, this is how we *will* be treated.

Nothing will help me more with my program today than to practice the Golden Rule, even in the face of trying situations. This will show me, more than words ever can, that God is really in charge of my life.

JUNE 18

AM I AN UNDERACHIEVER?

Lost Opportunities   We would be unusual among compulsive people if we hadn't missed out on opportunities. We might even view ourselves as underachievers who never reached our full potential.

Let's remember that the world is choked with people who haven't attained their potential, often for reasons beyond their control. This fact also must be known to our Higher Power, the author and grantor of all human gifts.

It may be that we achieve that to which we aspire when we follow a better way of life and become clean and sober. This could be God's will for us, with more blessings to follow. If our needs have been met, we may realize we have been as prosperous as we're supposed to be.

The true achievements most desperately needed today are in the spiritual realm. A rereading of *Alcoholics Anonymous* can help remind us of this.

I'll not waste any time fretting today about what I might have achieved if things had been different. I might already be one of the world's highest achievers if I'm living a spiritual life.

JUNE 19

OPEN-MINDED BUT CONCERNED

Responsibility Open-mindedness is a quality that helps us attract new ideas for our self-improvement. Oddly, many of us thought we were open-minded long before we ever considered a Twelve Step program.

We learned that what we considered open-mindedness was really indifference based on self-justification. It follows that people who are deep into selfish, compulsive behavior will appear to be open-minded and even very tolerant. This attitude is really the result of a desire to be accepted in spite of questionable behavior. It reflects no concern for others.

In living the program, we seek to cultivate true open-mindedness. This means being open to new ideas and opportunities, but also being concerned about others and taking care not to harm them.

Today I'll be open to what people are thinking and saying. I will be careful not to let my own prejudices keep me from viewpoints that will help me and others.

JUNE 20

I'M CAREFUL WITH MY TIME

Successful Living   A speaker told us one day that people who can't manage their time also have difficulty handling their money. We have even heard that "time is money."

Without becoming misers or scrooges, we have a responsibility to use time wisely—other people's time as well as our own. Many people who believe they are moral and upright are so careless about keeping appointments and dates that they force others to wait. This is essentially stealing another's time.

Being prompt and managing all of our time well is part of mature living. It's part of being a responsible, grown-up, caring person. If we've been guilty of poor management of our own time, we've probably been wasting other people's time as well.

I'll be careful and prompt in all appointments today. I'll not waste others' time by being late.

REMEMBER THE GOLDEN KEY

Living in the Spirit   Whenever trouble arises, the first thing to do is to turn it over to our Higher Power. We can take all necessary practical steps to solve a problem, but we don't need to decide what the answer may be. Do this, and you'll soon be out of your difficulty.

This is essentially the formula of the Golden Key as taught by Emmet Fox. It is also the core idea of Steps Three and Eleven. It is a manner of living one's life with the constant knowledge that a Higher Power is always part of it.

We should also condition ourselves to believe that our Higher Power has been with us all along and will continue to show us the way. Nothing depends on our being "spiritual" or "saintly" or perfect in behavior. With all our shortcomings, we are and ever will be children of God.

My Higher Power is always with me today, supplying whatever I need for the accomplishment of any good purpose.

JUNE 22

WHAT SHOULD BE A MEETING TOPIC?

Helping Others   Meeting discussions sometimes seem to drift far afield. This may lead to suggestions that we "stick to our purpose" or "get back to basics."

But we are always on the right track if we're bringing up thoughts, feelings, and behaviors that are of concern to recovering people. The real aim of Twelve Step activity is to maintain our new life after we've established ourselves in it. All sorts of problems should be faced and discussed.

However, we should avoid asking for information we can obtain elsewhere. "Where can I find a real estate agent?" is outside the area of a proper meeting discussion. On the other hand, "How can I get over my resentment over being forced to sell my house?" is just what we should be talking about.

Today I'll keep in mind that I have friends who will help me deal with thoughts and feelings. This knowledge is a source of comfort and guidance.

JUNE 23

FEELING GRATITUDE

Self-Improvement A mistaken view of gratitude is that we have a right to expect it from people we've helped. In reality, we benefit to the extent that we feel grateful.

The terms *gratitude* and *grace* are linked by a common root, the Latin word *gratus*, which means "pleasing" or "thankful." To feel grateful is to experience a state of grace. This immediately raises us to a higher level of personal dignity and well-being.

Why do we need to feel gratitude? One possible reason is that most compulsive illnesses, such as alcoholism and drug addiction, are intensely self-oriented. This selfishness destroys the soul and keeps us in a state of spiritual infancy and isolation, with concurrent arrogance and anger. We cannot afford to live in this condition.

Feeling gratitude—even when we are in difficulty—can release us from this bondage.

Today I'll go out of my way to feel gratitude, and I will express it to individuals. I know this is for my own good as well as the other person's.

JUNE 24

EXPRESSING GRATITUDE

Self-Improvement   How can we express gratitude when we feel it? We can begin by simply using the proper forms of courtesy at all times; this reminds us that we can't live without other people.

The best way to express gratitude, however, is to "pass on" the good that has come to us. This is more effective when we share ideas and experiences that have helped us on the way to self-improvement.

It's also a good idea to dismiss thoughts and statements that are forms of prideful boasting. Even telling people how hard we've worked for the Twelve Step program can detract from our gratitude. And never, under any circumstances, should we put others under obligation to us.

I'll discover ways to express my gratitude today. I'll know that my best way of doing it is to pass on good ideas to others.

TRANSFORMING GARBAGE

Handling the Past   Left to itself, nature takes ordinary garbage and transforms it into useful nutrients that help sustain life. It's usually poor human action that makes garbage a problem.

Our mental and emotional garbage takes the forms of bad memories, festering resentments, and useless regrets. We waste time berating ourselves and others about bad decisions and experiences that are behind us.

The magic of the Twelve Step program is that we can use it to transform this mental garbage into useful experience. A past mistake can become an asset when we share it with others. Pain and suffering can teach a lesson that helps all of us to grow. By forgiving others, a resentment can be turned into a friendship.

I'll resolve today not to worry about garbage any longer than it takes to identify it and release it to my Higher Power for transformation.

JUNE 26

LET IT HAPPEN

Easy Does It Student pilots learn a simple method for getting an airplane out of a stall: Release the stick forward, and the airplane rights itself. Continue to hold the stick back, and you cause a fatal spin.

Many times, we cling too tightly to conditions that could simply right themselves if we would only let go. Situations often work themselves out when we stop pushing and pulling too hard.

If we're living on a spiritual basis and following our Twelve Step program, lots of unpleasant conditions will clear up without any strain or struggle on our part. The secret, then, is to do our part and act prudently, but also to be willing to let things happen.

I'll remember today not to push or pull too hard to get my way. Things might work themselves out if I simply let natural forces work properly in every situation.

HAVE I EVER BEEN HELPED?

Unselfishness Sometimes we hear hard-luck stories by people who claim they never "had a single helping hand." Everybody was against them.

It's true that certain people have had more than their share of abuse and abandonment. But it's hard to believe that helping hands haven't been extended—acts of kindness, often made by selfless but ordinary people.

Our problem has been in recognizing such helping hands. Lost in self-pity, we could hardly have recognized help when it was given. Nor were we capable of giving constructive assistance to others.

Furthermore, if people were against us, we may have provoked it. Our task is to change our thinking about the past and to be grateful for the people who were kind to us.

I realize that there are kind and decent people who have helped me. There are many such people in the world, and I want to be one of them.

WHY IT WORKS

Confidence Twelve Step meetings often begin with a reading from the famous Fifth Chapter, "How It Works." We know that the program does work, but why? Is there a secret or magic to it?

The real reason the program works is neither secret nor magic. The program actually relies on ancient principles that always amaze people when they are employed: Help others, and you help yourself. Clean up your own house. Put your trust in God, not frail human beings or shaky institutions. Remove false gods such as alcohol and other drugs.

There may be additional reasons for the program's success, but these are enough for a start. The Twelve Step program does work.

I'll take comfort today in knowing that I'm walking in a way that has been tested and proven. The program works if I let it work.

JUNE 29

WE ARE NOT ALONE

Strengthening Belief   A famous scientist named Julian Huxley wrote a scholarly book called *Man Stands Alone.* Others have exalted the same idea, along with the belief that "old" religious faiths and dogmas hold us back. Once liberated from such outmoded beliefs, humankind supposedly could build its own paradise on earth.

Let the arguments go on, but the Twelve Step movement supports belief in a Supreme Intelligence and Power that works in human affairs. "No human power could have relieved our alcoholism" and "God could and would if sought" are powerful statements of our belief.

Our victory over alcohol proclaims that we are not alone and that our purpose in life is somehow part of an infinite purpose ceaselessly working within and around us. The best and highest answers to life's riddle will also come as we seek conscious contact with the power behind this purpose.

I'll never feel that I'm alone for a single minute today. My Higher Power is with me every step of the way.

MAKING ALL THINGS NEW

Releasing the Past A Twelve Step program should give us a new way of life, our friends often say. We should have new attitudes, new experiences, new opportunities.

If we're to grasp this new way of life, we must let go of the old habits of the past. No alcoholic can recover, for example, by choosing to remain in the old drinking environment. We must also "recover" from other relationships and patterns that were destructive or kept us from our highest good.

"Behold, I make all things new," is the ancient promise. As our thoughts and beliefs change, the old patterns drop away and the new life reveals itself to us.

Today I'll drop the negative or outworn relics from the past and press on to find the things that are for my highest good.

July

JULY 1

NEVER TOO LATE

Self-Expression Wasted time and lost opportunities were often the prices we paid for our problems. In recovery, some people feel they have no opportunity to do certain things because they're too old or the right time has passed.

This is all false belief, and part of it may grow out of the emphasis on youth, which seems to be greatly prized. We can't be young forever, but we can always have interests and enthusiasm. We can work to maintain good health and an optimistic outlook.

We can learn something new every day of our lives. We can feel good, we can launch new ventures, and we can try new ways to use our talents. It's never too late to be what we ought to be.

Whatever my age or place in life, I'll know today that wonderful opportunities for creative self-expression are all around me.

JULY 2

A SPIRITUAL LIFE IS NATURAL

Conscious Contact   Coming into what is clearly a spiritual program, we may have been fearful that our own unworthiness would hold us back. We may have believed that a spiritual life and a "conscious contact" with God are reserved for a few people with saintly qualities.

What we must know is that the spiritual life is every person's right. It includes the human qualities that have brought our greatest progress. "The spirit of the thing" is an ordinary phrase, but it expresses the presence of a Higher Power in our lives.

What's most useful to know is that we can contact our Higher Power at any time, in any place. This can be extremely important when we are in very bad situations. We always have a Higher Power to pull us through and to set things right in our lives. That's our birthright as human beings.

I'll turn to my Higher Power frequently throughout the day, if only for a few moments each time. This will keep me on the right path.

DON'T BE A VICTIM

Surviving Some people refer to us as victims of our problems, but we should not accept such labeling. A better term for us is *survivors*.

Working in step with our Higher Power, we should view ourselves as capable of rising above all the challenges and conditions that confront us. If we call ourselves victims, we'll soon be inviting more people and situations to victimize us. As survivors, however, we will always learn to sail through the roughest storms.

Looking at the general world situation, it does seem realistic to say that lots of people are victims. But we must always take into account the vast power that resides in every human soul. People have tremendous power to change their conditions, and when word of this finally gets around, we'll see a worldwide spiritual awakening that will change everything for the better.

Whatever I'm facing today, I'll know that the spirit within me also gives me the qualities I need to survive.

OUR COMMON KNOWLEDGE

Progress One guiding factor in Twelve Step groups is the sharing of experience and knowledge. The fact that a few people seem especially gifted as speakers and workers doesn't relieve us of the need for every person's participation.

Such group efforts are important to all human progress. For every outstanding person, there are hundreds who contribute to the success of any venture.

What we bring to the group is our experience as well as a strong commitment to the group's purpose. This makes our meetings warm, interesting, and helpful. The group can always be such a center if its members really are a part of it.

I'll remind myself today that I can draw strength from the group and also make it stronger with my participation.

WHAT BRINGS CHANGE?

Inventory In human affairs, vast changes sometimes take place almost spontaneously, bringing
on revolutionary upheavals. What brings about
such changes?

These visible changes, for good or bad, occur
because people come to accept new ideas. It's easy
to see how this works in one person's life, but it
works in the same way with societies.

The Twelve Step movement is a most dramatic
form of such change. We've become effective because we have new forms of thinking to replace
the old destructive forms that caused so much
harm. Our movement will grow and develop only
as long as we retain the new ways of thinking that
first brought about this change.

**I'll hold to the idea that my life can only be as
good as the thoughts I choose.**

JULY 6

SHOULD WE INTERVENE?

Recovery The method of conducting interventions is considered an effective way of confronting alcoholics and drug addicts. Interventions are done with the hope that this confrontation will "raise the bottom," and that the addict will face the condition before there's further anguish.

However effective interventions may be, they're not part of the Twelve Step program. Our work is based on attraction, not the admitted coercion that's part of intervention.

If we take part in interventions, this separation should be clearly understood. The person who still suffers should know that the Twelve Step program depends on attraction, not any of the other methods that might be available.

It's important to make this point clear, because the intervention may fail. Whether it does or not, the individual must not be left with the idea that intervention is a Twelve Step activity. At any stage, the fellowship is always available to him or her.

I'll probably see lots of people today who need help in facing their addiction. I'll know that their recovery comes in God's good time.

WHAT SHOULD I HAVE SAID OR DONE?

Second Thoughts After an intense discussion, we might rehash what we said and wish we'd said something else. Perhaps some brilliant remark occurs to us long after the conversation has ended.

We can say only what comes to us at the time of the discussion. Our best preparation for any such discussion—however important—is to place the matter in God's hands, seeking the highest good for everyone involved.

It may be that the brilliant thoughts coming to us later would have actually been inappropriate. After all, important discussions also involve exchanges of strong feelings that influence the meeting. If our feelings are in line with the high principles of the program, the discussion should go well. In such cases, we will probably say what we're supposed to say.

I'll do my best today without trying to second-guess every word or action.

GOD'S WILL FOR US

Spiritual Guidance "I was afraid God would want me to do something unpleasant, like go off to become a monk," a young man said at a Twelve Step meeting. "That's why I had a hard time seeking God's will for me."

This sort of comment is heard now and then at meetings. It reveals a belief that God is a harsh taskmaster who delights in imposing difficult conditions on us.

The truth is that God's purpose is to help us be more of what we ought to be, which is always something better than what we're experiencing now. Few people are ever called to be monks, but those who do are pleased with their choice and devote themselves to it.

We must always be interested in finding God's direction in our lives. It will turn out to be something far better than anything we could have planned.

I need not fear God's direction in my life. It's actually what I need in order to reach my true place.

WHAT IS THE REAL CAUSE?

Motivations Bringing her alcoholic husband home from a treatment center, a woman was dismayed when an argument ensued and he left the car in a rage. She blamed herself and their argument when he finally arrived home, drunk.

Seasoned veterans of alcoholic games will quickly understand that the argument had no part in "causing" the alcoholic to drink. Instead, the argument was something he started as a means of getting away from his wife. He still wanted and needed to drink.

In dealing with our compulsive illnesses, we must separate our excuses from what's really going on. Arguments do not cause alcoholics to drink, but they can be used as convenient devices for getting our way.

I must take responsibility for my own behavior. If I have chosen sobriety, no person and no event can cause me to drink.

FOOLISH RISKS

Maintaining the New Way There are only a few practices that really must be considered unacceptable for recovering people. AA even concedes, for example, that there's nothing wrong with having lunch with a friend in a bar if one's house is in order.

Under no circumstances, however, should recovering people do anything that puts their sobriety at risk. The stakes are too high. Recovery is too precious. The new life is too important.

What practices might come under the heading of risky? A dangerous one, common among young and old alcoholics alike, is returning to the old crowd that's still drinking and drugging. It's risky to associate with our former drinking lifestyles, and we'll recognize this if we're working our program.

Part of the honesty I'll practice today is knowing my own motives for everything I do.

FIGHTING THE PROBLEM

Recovery There are still large numbers of people who believe that alcoholism and other compulsions can be overcome if one simply has the determination to fight such problems. Most of us in recovery, however, never succeeded with this approach. That's because when we fight a problem, we tend to think about it all the time. We build it up in our minds so that it occupies most of our attention and then hits back at us.

The Twelve Step program uses a different approach. We focus our attention on recovery and the good ideas that go along with it. Our problem is always there, of course, but it no longer has the power to hurt us if we continue to focus on recovery instead of our addiction. We should also believe, as it's stated in the Big Book, that we're no longer fighting anything or anybody. Instead, we're letting the Power work in us and through us.

Not for a minute should I ever believe that I have the power to fight my addiction alone. That strength will come from my Higher Power as I continue to direct my attention to positive things.

PATS ON THE BACK

Self-Esteem   Recovery from a compulsive illness such as alcoholism often brings "pats on the back." This praise is a welcome change from the criticism our problems once raised.

We should accept such pats on the back graciously, but without taking the personal credit this sort of praise implies. We can become addicted to praise seeking, and we may even invite it as a way of building up self-esteem.

Moreover, much of our challenge is still ahead of us. The real victory may be in learning how to live after we've established our initial freedom. We learn that all human beings must face issues such as boredom and pain, which we tried to avoid with our drinking. We may get few pats on the back for our success in this everyday living, but our healthier lifestyle is reward enough.

If I receive praise today, I'll acknowledge it graciously, knowing that such praise is not necessary for my well-being.

SOLVING PROBLEMS IS THE PROOF

Spiritual Guidance Although we try, it's almost impossible for us to use logic to prove the existence (or nonexistence) of God. Our best proof of God's activity in our lives has to come from personal experience.

That's the message of the Twelve Step movement: God has done for us what we could not do for ourselves. We cannot be responsible for settling simmering religious and doctrinal issues that have been around for centuries. We can find our own help by following the example of others in the Twelve Step programs.

When spiritual guidance brings answers and solutions, we don't have to defend or justify our belief in our Higher Power. What better proof do we need than evidence that the program does work?

I'll follow my Higher Power today and then let the results speak for themselves.

SELF-ESTEEM IN RESPONSIBLE WORK

Self-Confidence "Whatever your hand finds to do, do it with all your might," goes an ancient saying. However long ago this was said, it applies to our work here and now.

Part of recovery lies in doing useful and satisfying work. We can't wait until the "perfect" job appears. Our success will come in doing the very best we can in our present situation. If we're unemployed, we can still be useful and active in ways that will help us find the right situation.

And as we work for a living, we'll find that another important benefit of our work will be greater self-esteem. We'll have more respect for ourselves as we continue to be both productive and active.

Whatever my job is, I'll give it my best today. I'll be grateful for having the opportunity to work productively.

JULY 15

THE POSSIBLE DREAM

Reaching Objectives Although we hear people ridicule the practice of daydreaming, we also hear them express admiration for people who pursued and realized their dreams. How do we know when we are pursuing the right dreams?

Useful, effective dreams may seem farfetched, but they still have a possibility of fulfillment. In some ways, they're tied to what we can do if we have the right opportunities and use our talents properly.

Fantasies, or useless dreams, can never happen. Fantasies are often based on our past and how it might have been different. It's also useless to fantasize about feats that are completely beyond anything we could ever do. These dreams are a waste of time and energy.

What's exciting, however, is that every person can find dreams that are possible and based on reality. It's important to pursue *these* dreams and bring them into realization.

I'll keep my realistic dreams very much alive today, knowing they're the patterns I need for reaching my long-term objectives.

JULY 16

ACCEPTING AND CORRECTING MISTAKES

Mature Living Being in error now and then is part of our human existence. Many of us, however, feel unbearable self-reproach when we make a mistake. Some compulsive people even blame themselves for errors beyond their control.

But the worst mistake is the refusal, or denial, of responsibility for mistakes. This comes from a strange belief that we can erase the mistake by refusing to accept it. It may stem from the belief that we should be above mistakes. This is immature thinking.

We are learning and growing when we accept our mistakes graciously and immediately move to correct them. Most of the time, when this is done, the distress passes quickly and we can go on to other matters.

I'll take full responsibility for all of my actions today, and I'll move quickly to correct any of my mistakes.

WE NEVER ARRIVE

Finding Happiness We delude ourselves if we believe that our happiness and well-being will come when we reach a certain goal. Whatever happiness and well-being we obtain must come through the process of living in ordinary, everyday situations.

If we observe carefully, we'll find lots of happy people who are in situations or work that we might consider unpleasant. It is not the work or situation that creates happiness and fulfillment. What counts is the attitude toward it.

Those of us in Twelve Step programs should have special insight into this issue of happiness. We tried to find it, here and now, in false ways. But it is available to us, here and now, in ordinary living.

I'll be happy today in knowing that I'm blessed with the ordinary tasks of life.

WHAT IS A NEW FREEDOM?

Release We're promised a "new freedom" in the Twelve Step program. How does this differ from the "old freedom" we've known?

The new freedom is an inner feeling of release from the bondage of compulsion. We are no longer serving as our own jailers. We are free from useless things that have held us back. Think of the burdens we had assumed by fearing others, by holding grudges, by having needless regrets.

This new freedom has nothing to do with political or civil liberties, which we hope to enjoy as our birthright. But nobody can give us freedom if we are locked into compulsions that bind us. We must seek the new freedom within ourselves.

Throughout the day, I'll think of myself as a completely free person. I'm free at last from the bondage I imposed upon myself.

HURRYING UP TO WAIT?

Practicing Serenity We often urge ourselves to hurry up when there's no good reason for it. At such times, all we really do is create needless tension and anxiety.

The slogan "Easy does it" is our answer to such calls to hurry. The slogan suggests that we simply move into the rhythms of life and "go with the flow."

It's not hurrying but steady effort that finally brings achievement. We've had entirely too much hurry and impatience. What we really need is confident, persistent effort in the right direction. We should be especially reminded of this when we see anxious, impatient people speeding through traffic only to be forced to wait at traffic lights, risking life and limb to save a few seconds. A good steady pace is what we need, and it will win the game.

I'll be active today, but not overactive. I'll look for rhythm and efficiency in everything I do.

A SENSE OF HIGHER POWER

Spiritual Guidance   If we go through the day with a confidence that our Higher Power is with us, events will go better than they would if we hadn't held to this belief. We will be more effective in everything we do. We will actually have more power in all activities.

This is what is meant in the Eleventh Step: "the power to carry that out." Knowing that the Higher Power is in our lives, we also find the power to do what we believe to be God's will for us. As this confidence strengthens and is seasoned by experience, it becomes part of our nature.

Eventually, we'll sense our Higher Power working in our lives. We can learn to accept this with the same sure belief that we accept the sun's rising and the changing of the seasons. And we'll have the power to do whatever must be done by us.

A conscious contact with God can raise my daily activities to higher levels, giving me the power of achievement.

CREATING GOOD IMPRESSIONS

Attitude   There's a saying that we have only **one** chance to make a good first impression. That's true, but we always have the opportunity to make good lasting impressions.

The secret of making good impressions is contained in one word: *attitude.* Whatever we really feel will be expressed to others as our true character, and the impression we give will be authentically us.

The way to control the impressions we are making is simply to continue cultivating an attitude that's consistent with humility, acceptance, and graciousness. We should have others' best interests at heart without being meddlesome. We should be genuinely helpful.

This attitude will create any good impressions we need to make.

Working to make sure I'm thinking the right way, I'll forget about the impression I'm making. If my attitude is right, the impression will take care of itself.

THE RIGHT PLACE FOR MY TYPE

The Right Work "You cannot change your type, but you can make yourself a brilliant success in that type," wrote Emmet Fox. This is a reminder for people who are discontented with their lot in life, and this includes most people who participate in Twelve Step programs.

There are many different "types" of people, and all types are good. We only need to find where our type is required and then do our best in that place. We will have immediate advantages, because all of our energies and talents will then be applied in the right way.

We should never spend a moment envying other types of people who are brilliantly successful in their activities. Our happiness is to be found in our place, not theirs.

If I'm doing what's right for my type, I'll give it my very best. If I'm in the wrong place, I'll know that my Higher Power is guiding me toward the right outlet for my talents.

SENSING REJECTION

Self-Esteem and Maturity We laugh when a recovering person tells how he "learned to quit just before he got fired." We sometimes can tell when a rejection is coming, and we take steps—such as quitting—to avoid further pain and humiliation.

In the recovery process, there still may be times when we sense a coming rejection. If it does come, we must remember that rejection is part of living. People receive rejection for all sorts of reasons, including wrong ones.

When we do sense any kind of a rejection in the works, our best course is to let it happen, accept it, and put it behind us. If we are living our program, we don't need to feel pain or humiliation, as rejection is simply part of normal human experience.

I'll try today to be as accepting as possible in everything I do. If others choose to reject me, I will also accept this without resentment or self-reproach.

OVERCOMING A BAD DISPOSITION

Temperament People with bad dispositions, like people with drinking problems, do not recognize how difficult they are. They accept their bad disposition as normal. Some people even declare proudly that they're in a bad mood until they've been awake several hours or have had three cups of coffee.

We do not have to put up with a bad disposition. If we find ourselves touchy or grumpy at times, we should immediately release this to our Higher Power. There is a better pattern of thought and feeling to replace anything that comes across to others as a bad disposition.

It's surprising to learn that we don't have to live with a bad disposition. What's even more surprising is that we'll also be happier and more relaxed without it.

A bad disposition, we learn, is just so much unnecessary baggage we don't have to carry.

I'll be relaxed and friendly at all times today. I have neither a need nor an excuse for a bad disposition.

DEALING WITH DISAGREEABLE PEOPLE

Personal Relations At every turn in the road, we're likely to meet disagreeable people, sometimes unexpectedly. Sometimes, we're forced to deal with them.

The Twelve Step program does not make this entirely painless, but it smoothes the process. One thing we've learned is not to react with anger and contempt when we meet a disagreeable person, because such feelings on our part will only set off an explosion.

The Twelve Step program shows us how to give the "soft answer which turns away wrath." It will not be us, but our Higher Power who does the work. In time, we will respond in this way naturally. This is not cowardice—it is really another courageous way of dealing with human weaknesses.

I'll be calm and controlled today, no matter who or what comes into my life. My Higher Power supports me in my responses.

GUIDANCE IS ALWAYS MORAL

Spiritual Direction   History and even some modern experience prove that human beings can do terrible things while attributing their acts to "following the will of God." How can this be, if God is the source of all true morality?

True guidance from our Higher Power will always be in line with the best principles we know. Lying, stealing, murder—these come out of the human heart, not the heart of God.

Some people justify wrong actions by pointing to the way things work among animals in the wild. But we are not animals in the wild, and we have a destiny that can be reached only by learning and practicing higher standards.

Wrong action is never God's guidance for us. It's always a lower human nature trying to justify the old selfishness.

Whatever I do today will be morally correct if I truly seek and follow God's guidance.

NO TAP DANCING AROUND PROBLEMS

Inventory Our program calls for a "searching and fearless" moral inventory, not only in the beginning, but as we continue to follow our new way of life.

What this means is complete honesty about who and what we really are. We should not tap-dance around our problems in order to evade responsibility. This will not bring the cleansing we need for real sober living. We need deep changes, not mere surface ones.

Difficult as it is to be fully honest, it's made easier when we remind ourselves that it's all for our own recovery. We benefit in proportion to the amount of honesty we bring to our inventory. If it's searching and fearless, the results will be far-reaching and substantial.

I will not shirk from facing the truth about myself as I go through the day. What I need for self-improvement will be revealed to me.

THE TRUE SECURITY

Security We can feel insecure for many reasons, but the fundamental reason is that we do not have a firm anchorage in our Higher Power. This anchorage must be our true security, and it is really the only form that can survive any attack.

Regardless of who we are, we can know and feel that our Higher Power is guiding and directing us at all times. If we find ourselves being threatened by a person or situation, we can deal with it by knowing that our Higher Power is in charge of all outcomes. If we envy somebody, we must get back to an acknowledgment of God as the source of everything.

If we feel inadequate around people who seem to be immensely self-confident and secure, we should not try to imitate their manner and behavior. Rather, we should simply put our trust in our own Higher Power, and our feeling of true security will express itself in proper ways.

All the things we view today as being secure are probably only temporary. Our true security can come only from God.

JULY 29

FLATTERY OR PRAISE?

Human Relations   Flattery and praise are social lubricants that serve human purposes. But flattery is merely manipulative, while genuine praise is beneficial to everybody.

Many of us with troubled backgrounds also have trouble giving and accepting praise. Sometimes we mistake flattery for praise and use it either to manipulate others or allow ourselves to be manipulated. Perhaps we're either too proud or too self-conscious to deal with real praise.

Another mistake is in believing that praise should be given out only sparingly, only after outstanding achievement. Not so. We need to give and receive praise continuously in order to reach higher levels of achievement. Knowing its importance, we'll also learn how to avoid flattery.

I'll offer both verbal and silent praise today in my dealing with others. We'll all benefit from it.

FOUNDERS WITH CLAY FEET

Sound Thinking With any organization or society, the time comes when people find fault with the founders. The faults of these pioneering leaders are examined and perhaps even used to discredit them.

Founders are only human beings, and they are likely to exhibit the human shortcomings all of us have. If these founders turn out to have clay feet, perhaps the fault is ours for idolizing them in the first place.

The real role of a founder is to lay the foundation for further building. Unless the society grows, improving over what the founder had in mind, it is not likely to survive. Its real work should be to surpass the founder so as to be of greater service to others.

I'll be careful not to put anyone on a pedestal and then complain about his or her clay feet.

GROUP INTELLIGENCE

Getting Ideas "All of us know more than any one of us" is a saying that applies to Twelve Step groups. No matter how much experience any single individual has, it's surpassed by the collective knowledge of the group.

That's a good reason in itself for drawing upon these groups, and there are others as well. We need the pool of intelligence that the groups build up over time. We need the group's strength when our own is waning.

We also learn help that comes in surprising ways. The person in the group who seems least knowledgeable may express an idea that is just what we need at the time.

The group can meet many of our needs if we give it a chance. Regular attendance at meetings will keep us in touch with the group's ideas.

I'll stay in touch today with ideas that come from members of my group. Joined together, we have lots of knowledge.

August

AUGUST 1

WHO IS SINCERE?

Sincerity We sometimes dismiss other people's relapses with the explanation that they didn't really want to stay sober or that they lacked sincerity of purpose.

We have no way of gauging just how sincere anybody really is. Even in trying to understand ourselves, we may detect traces of the double-mindedness that got us into trouble. Even if we've been sober for years, the old desire to drink can be lurking somewhere in the back of our minds. It's wise to assume that this is so even when there's no conscious desire to drink. If hidden desires to drink still persist even after years of sobriety, it points to the persistence of the disease—not to one's insincerity.

It may even be that sincerity, like sobriety, has to be sought on a daily basis. Perhaps we are capable of being sincere today, and then lapse into insincerity tomorrow. To accept this is a sign of prudence and maturity, and perhaps even a measure of humility.

I'll seek to be sincere today about the things that really count. If I know I'm insincere in certain areas, I'll seek more understanding about it.

"THAT'S THE WAY I AM"

Getting Better Bad behavior is sometimes justified as a form of self-expression: "That's the way I am." Others are supposed to tolerate this or risk losing a friendship.

In our program, we should modify any behavior that offends or hurts others. If we have been too brutally frank in our comments, for example, maybe we're at fault. What we call honesty is really a form of cruelty.

If we persist in "being the way we are" even when it doesn't work, we have nobody to blame but ourselves when things go wrong. Other people are entitled to be treated fairly and decently, just as we want to be. Perhaps "the way I am" is something that can be changed for the good of all, ourselves included.

If I have habits and traits that cause friction with others, I'll take a new look at them. It's possible that this is something I can and should change.

WATCHING OUT FOR PEER PRESSURE

Maintaining Sobriety   It's said that peer pressure often draws young people into alcoholism and drug addiction. As adults following a recovery program, we also are susceptible to peer pressure.

At a cocktail reception, for example, some people may express mild pity that we're having "only soft drinks," as if we're doing a form of penance. Or they may express exaggerated admiration for our success in recovery. Even this can make us feel different.

We need not be critical of such reactions. The fact is that we *are* somewhat different when we're staying sober in situations where excessive drinking is normal.

We should not, however, make this our problem if others draw attention to it. This is peer pressure, but we should be mature enough to dismiss it.

Whatever situation I'm in today, if I know I'm on the right path, I'll not be swayed by the opinions and comments of others. Their opinions cannot affect me if I know I'm doing the right thing.

TREATING LOVED ONES
WORSE THAN STRANGERS

Personal Relations   Some of us grew up with resentments about the way our families treated us. It was confusing to notice how nice our parents could be toward strangers and then how abruptly they could become abusive toward us.

The best release for this kind of resentment is forgiveness, but we should also ask ourselves if we're guilty of the same faults. Are we discourteous and inconsiderate toward our own children and family members? Do we apologize when we offend strangers, but not when we hurt our own children?

We should try to treat everyone with fairness and kindness. No family member should be subjected to our incessant criticism and rudeness. We owe them the same courtesies we extend to strangers.

If I've had bad examples of abusive treatment in my own early years, I'll change the pattern by treating my own family with fairness and kindness, starting today.

CAN WE FIX
OTHER PEOPLE'S PROBLEMS?

Problem Solving In Twelve Step work, we never run out of people who face serious problems. We're often tempted to use our own expertise and resources to fix these problems for others.

This can be a mistake. It is always risky to undertake such assignments without a great deal of thought and understanding. Such attempts to fix others usually deal only with symptoms rather than causes.

Unless another person is totally helpless, the best course is to share experiences and knowledge with others, but to leave the problem solving to them. We should not encourage anyone to become dependent on us, nor should we set ourselves up as godlike individuals who have all the answers. We actually may be showing off instead of helping, and we may also be robbing others of the self-confidence and growth that come from fixing their own problems.

I'll share my experiences and hope today, while refraining from trying to fix people. I don't have answers for everybody, and it's wrong to believe I do.

AM I SPECIAL?

Self-Understanding An early professional believed that alcoholics got into trouble because they thought they were "special." Thinking we're special certainly creates all sorts of problems.

It's true that every person is special in that no two people are exactly alike. But we're also part of the human race, and we are bound by the general limitations that apply to everyone. We got into trouble partly because we thought we were special and could break universal commonsense rules.

When we stop thinking of ourselves as special, we also become more teachable. We learn more from the experiences of others. Then we realize that we're both special and generic, and we use this knowledge for self-improvement rather than self-destruction.

I'll remember today that I'm special in certain ways, but that I'm also part of the human race and subject to things that apply to everyone.

COMPETING WITH OTHERS

Attitude Some of us never liked close competition. We preferred to be clear winners or not to compete at all. We didn't like to have competitors breathing down our necks.

This attitude kept us from doing our best, and we made a mistake when we thought we were competing with others. We're actually competing with ourselves at all times, trying to do better than we did yesterday. The presence of other people only helps us to set performance standards and goals.

Once we accept the idea of self-improvement, we can delight in competition. We can take satisfaction in situations where, though we were not number one, we came in a close second instead of a sullen last.

I'll know today that I'm always working with others but only competing against myself.

AUGUST 8

NO SELF-DECEPTION

Honesty Most of the time, other people don't really deceive us. We deceive ourselves by refusing to face life realistically. We often believe false information simply because we want to believe it.

Living on a Twelve Step basis should enable us to face reality without becoming cynical or pessimistic. If a friend appears to be lying to us, for example, we can accept this as a single lie, not as a complete betrayal. In addition, we learn not to lie to ourselves. This helps us avoid shaky business schemes and unrealistic hopes.

At the same time, we can still retain our capacity for believing in wonders and miracles. We have experienced enough miracles to prove that they really happen.

I'll use my head as much as possible today to help keep my heart from getting me into trouble, but I'll remember that it's what's in my heart that counts.

AUGUST 9

CONFIDENCE IN THE NEXT PHASE

Assurance "God has carried me this far. I will not be let down now." These are brave words of recovering people who find themselves facing new doubts and fears.

There's nothing unrealistic about this attitude. Those of us in Twelve Step programs are beneficiaries of a miraculous chain of events that brought our movement into being. Our responsibility is to continue carrying the message by proving how the program works.

It's our success in dealing with life's problems that eventually attracts others to our fellowship. The best proof of how our spiritual program works is showing how our Higher Power continues to solve problems in our lives.

We don't always know what the next phase in our lives will bring. We can only know that with God, all sorts of wonderful things continue to be possible.

Though I can't see around the corner, I'll know today that my Higher Power will guide me smoothly and safely through the next phase.

CAN'T OR WON'T?

Willingness   "I can't do it," a person declared as the meeting opened. "I simply can't stop drinking." That launched the evening's discussion as thirteen people offered their ideas and suggestions.

One idea that emerged was that *can't* was really *won't*. The individual was still holding back on recommended actions, such as attending more meetings and making excuses for not doing so. It became clear that the quest for sobriety was still only half-hearted.

In dealing with a powerful addiction, we learned long ago that half-hearted approaches don't work. That's why willingness is called the key to recovery. If the "won't" factor isn't eliminated, our chances for recovery are very poor.

Some people recognize their "won't" attitude but still desire sobriety. For them, the answer is to continue attending meetings and doing the other things that bring sobriety. This can result in a breakthrough when they least expect it.

I'll remember today that *can't* is often *won't*. If I'm not taking the right steps to help myself, I'll check myself for willingness.

WHAT IS REAL OPEN-MINDEDNESS?

New Ideas   When we're urged to be open-minded, what's really involved? Open-mindedness certainly can't mean accepting every idea that comes down the road, because some of them are worthless or harmful.

Open-mindedness really means a readiness to put our deeply held opinions aside long enough to consider new ideas. If we simply refuse to listen to anything new, we'll avoid the bad ideas, but we'll also miss out on the ideas that can help us.

If we're really honest, we can look back to see many ideas that helped us after we reluctantly agreed to consider them. It's important to screen ideas as they come to us, but we can't block them out completely. All a good idea needs to help us is a fair chance.

I'll work at being more open-minded today. It's possible I've been blocking out ideas that could help me.

THINGS I CAN'T FIX

Acceptance   One of the sad realities of life is that we're awash in disorder that we can't fix. All around us, the world seethes and festers with ailments and injustices that are beyond our control.

We can react by becoming angry or by making quixotic efforts to solve some of these problems. Our best course, however, is to apply our Twelve Step program to life in this world. The Serenity Prayer suggests we accept what we can't change. A slogan reminds us to set priorities ("First things first"). The Eleventh Step remind us to always seek God's will.

This will enable me to live effectively while doing my best to serve others. In time, I may even discover that I can fix a few of the seemingly insoluble problems around me.

I'll realize today that I have the ability only to do certain things within my sphere of experience. I'll see to it, however, that I do these things well.

AUGUST 13

BLAMING OTHERS

Commonsense Action   No matter what happens, some people insist that a culprit must be found when things go awry. Someone must be blamed for every wrong or catastrophe.

We must be careful not to buy into this practice in three ways: First, we must avoid being held responsible for problems we didn't cause. Second, we must also avoid any personal guilt for such problems. Third, we must not fall into the trap of unfairly blaming other people.

The best use of the energy we spend hunting down culprits is to fix what's within our powers, to have "the courage to change the things [we] can." Then we will have done what we can to reduce the number of problems in the world while putting our own talents and energies to their best uses.

I'll keep some balance today if I hear anybody blaming others for the world's woes. We'll probably fix most problems one day at a time, and I'll do the best I can with those problems I know something about.

WASTING TIME

Time Management In dealing with our personal shortcomings, we may find traits of immaturity. For example, we might waste time doing the things we like to do rather than the things we must do.

We sometimes find a way to justify this. Drinking coffee with friends might be called "having a meeting" even when it goes far beyond normal limits and uses up time that should be devoted to family and work responsibilities.

Without becoming workaholics or drudges, we do need to be honest about our habits. If we're wasting too much time, it could be at the expense of things that need to be attended to promptly. When we waste time, we often have to work twice as hard to catch up later on.

Let's be honest about the management of our time.

I'll watch how I spend my time today. If I'm spending too much time socializing, I'll put myself on a reasonable schedule that balances both leisure and work.

DO WE HAVE A LARGER PURPOSE?

Peace The Twelve Step program came out of a movement that was attempting to save the world by establishing universal peace. Our purpose is scaled down to helping the person who still suffers.

We don't really know the route to world peace, but we have learned that we must be at peace with ourselves and others in order to live happily. This means releasing the old resentments, distrust, and other faults that plague so many of us.

Living the Twelve Step way might have been our first experience in getting along with others. We found it totally different from the hate and suspicion that once poisoned our lives and kept us in bondage.

At some point, we may also find that we're playing a part in the larger purpose of finding peace. We have, at least, removed ourselves from the raging conflicts that cause so much trouble in the world.

I'll be at peace with everyone I meet today. I've forgiven others and myself, and I'll do nothing today that gets me embroiled in conflict with others.

WHO IS A KEY PERSON?

Respecting Others   The Twelve Step movement grew out of a society that practiced a "key person" strategy: If you could win "important" people into your group, others of high standing would follow.

The experience of Alcoholics Anonymous led to a different strategy: Work with anybody who wants help, and let leaders appear as they will. The leaders, whom we call "trusted servants," were sometimes very ordinary people in the eyes of the world. Some were like Bill W., people of great ability whose careers had been wrecked by alcoholism.

In any case, it is obvious that we are poor judges of who might become a "key person." In the sight of God, we're told, all humans are equal. Our best success comes when we treat every newcomer as a "key person."

I'll remember today to view every person with the respect and consideration that is usually extended to people whom the world considers important.

WHOM SHOULD WE RESPECT?

Respecting Others   While having dinner in a nice restaurant, my friends and I realized that we were treating the young man bussing the table with cold indifference. He appeared to be unsure of himself, doing his work with apprehension and a lack of confidence.

Here was an example of a person who needed silent encouragement. He needed to be assured that his performance of honest, useful work was respected and appreciated. He also needed to be reminded that he had opportunities to continue developing and using his talents. Perhaps we, as patrons of the restaurant, could provide that.

Sometimes this encouragement can simply be expressed in the way we act and feel toward people. If it is genuine and based on good spiritual principles, it will be understood. It's actually a form of practicing the principles of the Twelve Steps in all our affairs. At the same time, we practice identifying with every person we meet.

I'll try to take note of every person I come in contact with today, knowing that everyone needs support and encouragement. I can do my part to provide that.

HANDLE TODAY'S PROBLEM

Living Today   Many of us face seemingly insurmountable difficulties, perhaps because of our compulsion or simply through misfortune. Whatever the scale of our problems, "One day at a time" and "First things first" are keys to handling them.

Today, we can deal only with today's problems. One of today's problems, of course, may be worrying about the future. A good method of handling that problem is to turn our concern about it over to our Higher Power.

But when we do have work that clearly should be done today, we must carry through with it. It's neither reasonable nor sensible to put off things that we can and should do today.

There are certain tasks and responsibilities that must be dealt with today. I will not put them off.

AUGUST 19

INVENTORY IS NOW

Personal Inventory   In the early days of AA, the dramatic accounts of drinking escapades seemed to show honesty. Taking personal inventory often included telling others about bizarre behavior connected with drinking.

We know today that inventory ought to continue on a daily basis, even though years have passed since our last drink. We've learned through painful experiences that in sobriety we can still display many of the shortcomings that plagued us as practicing alcoholics.

It can also be a trap to focus on our past wrongs rather than today's faults. We may be using this focus on the past to avoid being honest about where we stand today.

Let's remember that inventory is always *now*. Taking inventory of the past won't help us with today's shortcomings.

I won't use a discussion of my past wrongs as a subterfuge to keep from being honest about today's wrongs. I'll continue to take personal inventory and admit wrongs as they come up.

ALL THAT GLITTERS

Tempting Moments   Though real sobriety means all loss of desire to drink, it's not uncommon to have moments when the old life takes on a sudden appeal.

This appeal is never based on a realistic look at things as they were. It is more a rush of feeling connected with some alluring aspect of the drinking life.

Such a false feeling will always pass if we let ourselves remember what happened to us and why we needed to seek recovery. We cannot have this rush of feeling when we remember the misery, despair, and other pain from that part of our lives.

"All that glitters is not gold," goes an old saying. All the glittering scenes connected with drinking are not really golden moments, either. They are, for us, always preludes to disaster.

I'll remember today to let realistic thinking rule my life even if there are moments when my feelings run temporarily awry.

MEETING NEEDS IN THE RIGHT WAY

Self-Understanding Bizarre as it is, the bad behavior of drunkenness has an underlying logic when it's really understood. Why, for example, would people squander money buying drinks for total strangers when their families are going without?

This is an insane way of meeting needs for intimacy and approval. It's true that these needs will never be met in this fashion, but try telling that to a person who is still drinking!

In recovery, we can more easily forgive ourselves for past actions when we realize they came out of a misguided attempt to meet basic needs. A starving person will seek out garbage. Starved as we were for the necessities of life, we sought a form of garbage. The good news in AA recovery is that sobriety will help us meet basic needs in the right way.

I'll keep in mind today that as a human being, I have certain needs that should be met in proper ways.

WHOSE EXPERIENCE IS IMPORTANT?

Sharing   In the Twelve Step movement, we often feature outstanding speakers at large anniversary meetings. In some ways, this makes celebrities of them—their personal stories seem to be deemed more important than those of others.

We should accept such large meetings for what they are: part entertainment, part socialization, and part celebration. The real work of our fellowship, however, lies in ordinary, continuous activity in the groups.

The most important experience to be shared is not the dramatic or humorous account heard at the large meeting. What really works to keep us sober is the experience we share with each other. This can survive long after the powerful speech is forgotten.

I'll remember today that I can find help and growth in talking with the different people I meet at regular meetings.

PLANNING FOR OTHERS

Letting Go   There are times when we think we see perfectly what others ought to be doing. It pains and disturbs us when loved ones—our children, perhaps—do not heed our advice.

In planning for others, we can easily fall into the trap of enabling. An enabler is a person who supports others in an unhealthy addiction or dependency.

We must not plan the lives of others, no matter how dear they are to us or how attached we become to them. They must have the freedom to live without obligation or the belief that they could not have succeeded without our help.

Freedom of choice is a precious right that includes the freedom to make mistakes.

I'll release any tendency I have to plan for others. At all times, my responsibility is to keep on the right track and let others be free.

IS LIFE UNFAIR?

Justice The glib remark "Life is unfair" is sometimes used to dismiss any concern about trouble or seeming injustice. This usually implies that all such matters are part of God's plan—that somehow God couldn't create life without making it unfair.

But nobody really knows whether life is unfair or not, since what we see is only a small part of it. We should know, however, that we can practice fairness ourselves. We will live better if we forget how unfair life can be and make the best of the opportunities we have.

Some of us could even argue that life treated us unfairly by giving us a susceptibility to alcoholism. In the long run, this turned out to be an opportunity to live the Twelve Step program. Some of us even consider this to be an outworking of divine justice that has proved to be eminently fair. As one AA member put it, "It was a case of one of the worst things becoming one of the best things that ever happened to me!"

I'll not let any seeming unfairness or injustice keep me from doing my best today. My real belief is that there is an eternal justice underlying all things.

WHAT SHOULD WE ACCEPT?

Acceptance Alcoholics usually have trouble accepting ordinary setbacks and limitations that other people live with all the time. Sometimes it seems much easier to just get drunk than to accept boredom and frustration.

The irony of such behavior is that we then have to accept much more failure as a result of problems created by drinking. Our drinking brings far more pain than it removes.

Learning acceptance in sobriety is part of the growing-up process. Along with learning to accept things we cannot change, however, we learn there are some things we don't have to accept. Living sober gives us the power and confidence to make such changes.

I'll repeat the Serenity Prayer today if I begin to feel disturbed or threatened. I will face life realistically while knowing I have many opportunities for growth and change.

WASTE UTILIZATION

Releasing the Past Today the world faces seemingly insurmountable problems with solid and liquid waste. Communities struggle to find solutions as waste accumulates and space for disposal sites grows scarce.

As recovering people, we have a similar problem with waste residues from our past. We don't seem to be able to bury bad memories; like the physical waste in the environment, they come back to poison us.

The best answer is to use waste, not throw it away. Instead of trying to bury the past, let's keep it in view but let it be purified by the sunlight of honesty and humility. By admitting past wrongs and forgiving everyone involved—including ourselves—we turn waste into useful experience. Nature can do this with much physical waste, over time. We can also let our spiritual nature do that with the emotional and mental waste of our past.

I'll realize that every past mistake and experience can be properly utilized today for something good and uplifting.

FINDING OUR REAL SELVES

Building Self-Esteem   Many of us sold ourselves short while we were drinking. We wanted approval and acceptance, but often felt unworthy of it, even accepting the unfavorable opinions others had toward us. We resented such opinions, but secretly feared that our critics were right.

In the Twelve Step program, however, we discover a higher and better self that hadn't found expression during active drinking. We no longer have to impress anybody, we no longer need applause, and we no longer crave the false camaraderie that passes for friendship among problem drinkers. We can, in many ways, become new people.

When we experience such change and growth, we may come to wonder how we ever could have been so deluded by the sick self of our drinking years. We feel relief when we realize that we no longer have to live and think that way—if we continue in the program and make sobriety our highest priority. We will realize too that the self we find in sobriety is the *real* self—a person who was there all along but was crowded out and suppressed by the demands of our sick nature. This real self is what we were created to be, and sobriety brought its discovery.

I'll go about my affairs today knowing that my real self is what God wants me to be. Being sober, I can now find answers and opportunities that were beyond my reach when I was still drinking.

NO PRAYER GOES UNANSWERED

Guidance It would be nearly impossible to do an accounting of the results of prayer. Sometimes there seems to be no answer, and at other times, an answer seems to be the result of coincidence. It's too easy to dismiss these results as things that would have happened even if we hadn't prayed.

Yet those of us who believe in prayer feel that it is indeed a way of communicating with our Higher Power. It takes many forms. Even thinking about God is a type of prayer.

The best answers to prayer come in the new ways we begin to feel about ourselves and others. If prayer brings us to a realization of being in tune with our Higher Power, we are working in the right way. The proper changes will come into our lives as needed. We should not try to "measure" results, because this tends to bring doubt into the process. Our only responsibility is to pray and then let God's work take place in our lives.

I will pray regularly today, thinking often about God and asserting to myself and others that this Higher Power is in charge.

AUGUST 29

GIVING THE RIGHT SUPPORT

Carrying the Message   We're surrounded by people who need help—financial and otherwise. It is sometimes tempting to believe that we can and should reach out to improve the conditions of their lives.

This is not always an easy thing to do, or even a right thing to do. The early AA members who tried this finally decided to limit most of their help simply to carrying the Twelve Step message. While this seemed callous, it was really the only practical approach to a difficult problem.

Many people are able to solve their own financial problems when they really understand and practice the Twelve Step program. If they still need other assistance, it is then given and received in ways that work.

In any case, we should always seek guidance and direction from our Higher Power when considering or offering any kind of assistance. We'll then know that any support we give will be the right kind.

I'll be willing today to assist others in any way I can. I will not, however, take responsibility for running their lives.

THE MASKS ARE FALLING

Openness Individuals and families can be quite successful at masking personal problems and feelings. This doesn't always work very well with alcoholics, though some of us did manage to conceal our problem for long periods before our lives began to break down. However, it is becoming more acceptable to admit to such problems, and it is no longer surprising to read that a prominent person is being treated for an addiction.

This new openness has also made it possible to abandon the masks we've been wearing to hide our feelings. When people learn they can be more open with their problems and need for help, it also becomes easier to admit that they are angry, fearful, unhappy, or even frightened.

Removing our masks and letting others see us as we are is only the first phase in the real honesty we're seeking. After expressing ourselves authentically, do we find we like who we are? Now that we know and admit the truth about ourselves, what are we going to do to make needed changes?

I will face who and what I really am today. I will use my strengths and not let any shortcomings keep me from being effective.

HONESTY IS NOT ENOUGH

Action   AA tells us that we must be honest about our problems if we hope to overcome them. Some people seem quite willing to do this. But an honest admission alone does not solve our problems. We have to go beyond honesty by taking needed action to correct what's wrong in our lives.

For example, we would not believe that anything had been corrected simply because a doctor diagnosed a physical problem. We know that such diagnosis is only a preliminary step that must lead to treatment to be effective. In the same way, an honest admission of our alcoholism does not lead to sobriety unless we take further action to address the problem.

We should also be careful about becoming prideful in announcing our shortcomings. If we are recovering from alcoholism but excuse a bad temper as one of our "alcoholic defects," are we attempting to correct our behavior? The more prideful we are about any fault, the more difficult it will be to change it.

Having become honest about my shortcomings, I'll look for opportunities today to make needed corrections in my behavior. If I find myself using my "alcoholic nature" as an excuse for unacceptable behavior, I'll take action to do something about it.

September

SEPTEMBER 1

ARE WE VICTIMIZING OURSELVES?

Finding the New Happiness Some believe that people create their own trouble by attracting the wrong conditions and people in their lives. This may not be entirely true, but we can find that some element of it was at work with us. Time and time again during our drinking, we set ourselves up for abuse and rejection, though our motives seemed right.

Why did we do this? Supposedly to punish ourselves, the theory has it. If this is true, then we should now call a halt to the process immediately. If we've emerged from the terrors of alcoholism, we've had all the punishment anybody needs.

We can change our bad patterns by looking carefully at the people and situations we seem to attract. Without resentment or condemnation, we can part company with any problems these have been bringing us. We can start building new relationships and attracting better conditions that will be immensely successful in terms of happiness and well-being.

I'll remember today that in the new life I'm seeking, there's no need for punishment. I will not go out of my way to attract people or conditions that create problems in my life.

SEPTEMBER 2

GOING WITH THE FLOW

Problem Solving   It's surprising how many problems solve themselves when we're willing to turn them over to our Higher Power. This isn't a self-fulfilling prophecy brought about by superstitious beliefs; we can actually find proof of this seemingly providential activity in our lives.

We don't have to convince anybody except ourselves that this process works. What we can prove is that some of our best opportunities come about by what we would call chance or coincidence. Indeed, the first meeting of the two AA founders could be called such a chance event.

We need to believe that our Higher Power is working ceaselessly for the upward development of the human race, and Twelve Step programs can be essential forces in this upward development. In our own lives, we can go with this flow of ever-increasing good, as we continue to feel ourselves a part of it.

I will not wrestle with every problem today. Some problems will be dealt with later and some will seem to solve themselves. I will know that I am part of an upward development that is continuing.

SEPTEMBER 3

WHAT IS POSSIBLE?

Spiritual Power "With God, all things are possible," goes an old saying. Yet most of us haven't seen any evidence of doing the impossible.

But through our program, we have truly accomplished things that we had considered nearly impossible at one time. "No human power could have relieved our alcoholism," we read in the AA Big Book. How many more conditions are we accepting because no human power—particularly ours—can relieve them?

As we grow in sobriety, we should continuously reinforce our belief that God is living and working in our lives. The "impossible" problems we'll need to work on will have roots in our own habits and feelings, but even if one of these deeply rooted problems has gone on for years, we need not despair of finding an answer.

If we persist in prayer and in turning the problem over to our Higher Power, an answer must come. It is never too late to find the changes we need and deserve.

Even if I haven't solved all my problems, I'll take the position today that correct solutions exist in the mind of God. I'll be open to signs that changes are coming.

SEPTEMBER 4

WHAT DO WE DESERVE?

Good Expectations We hear about people who snatch defeat from the jaws of victory. Some of us do that even in sobriety, experiencing failure just as success seems imminent.

At times, we may just be suffering from a bad situation that is all around us. But if we do seem to be having one bad break after another, we should look more carefully within ourselves for causes. We may be punishing ourselves, or pushing away our good simply because we do not feel worthy of it.

If we discover that this process is working in our lives, we must begin changing these false patterns immediately. Having forgiven ourselves and others, and having made amends, we need no punishment. We will work to succeed in all of our activities, with a reasonable expectation of success most of the time. We will expect and deserve the best.

I'll carry with me today a belief that I deserve to succeed and will take all necessary action to earn my success.

SEPTEMBER 5

BATTLES WE'VE WON OR LOST

Achievements Even the continuous sobriety we're enjoying is no shield from traps we seem to set for ourselves. At times, we can find ourselves in the foolish game of continuing to fight battles we've won or lost.

One losing battle is the attempt to win the approval of someone who has always disliked us. That person may be gone, but we still fight—and lose—the same battle when we find ourselves in a similar situation.

We also may have won some battles without knowing it. This can happen when we've set our goals unrealistically high. We may be fairly successful in our work, for example, but still feel that we have failed because a high goal we set eluded us. That goal, however, may have been all but impossible to attain, and while we mourn our perceived failure, we ignore the successes we may have achieved in the meantime. Consequently, we should never let any of these battles interfere with our plan for sobriety. We must stay sober at all costs.

This day, I'll not strive to impress people who may always disapprove of me. I will also accept my successes even if they fall short of my highest dreams.

SEPTEMBER 6

CHANGE IS SOMETIMES NECESSARY

Improvement Despite the fact that many of us live turbulent, chaotic lives, we may find in sobriety that we don't like change. This causes us to seek our security in familiar places, rather than reach out for the unknown that lies ahead.

This may not be real security, however, because familiar places and situations also change. Our resistance to change may simply be the fear of trying something new.

If we find that fear of change is causing us to put up with a situation that's become unsatisfactory, we need to adjust our attitude toward it. While we view change as risky, it may be the necessary route for improvement. Let's start by simply accepting the idea that change is sometimes necessary. After that, we can expect our Higher Power to guide us to the new situations that are right for us.

Today I may find myself fearing change. I'll remind myself that nothing ever stays the same, and that only change can bring the true good I'm always seeking.

SEPTEMBER 7

A NEW APPROACH TO FREEDOM

Staying Sober   Most of us discover that we've had mixed-up ideas about the nature of freedom. Real freedom is not simply doing exactly as one pleases; *privileges* would be the correct term for that. And desirable as political freedom is, it cannot give us what we're really seeking.

We should approach freedom by recognizing that we're really seeking release from the bondage of self. This self-concern can be one of the worst tyrannies humans face.

As we are released from the bondage of self, we learn that our choices begin to multiply. We make wise decisions instead of being driven to certain actions. We are truly free.

Today I'll enjoy a freedom that is available to anybody who seeks it wholeheartedly. I'll know it as the freedom only God can offer.

ADMITTING A WRONG

Inventory It is all but impossible for some people to make the simple admission, "I was wrong." We might have a problem with such admissions because we tend to believe that they place us at a disadvantage.

The reality is that the sooner we can admit a wrong, the more rapidly it can be corrected and put behind us. The refusal to admit a wrong means making more of the same mistakes, thus bringing further harm to ourselves and others.

We may have trouble admitting a wrong because we once faced excessive punishments when we were found wrong. We can find our true course by realizing that admission of our wrongs is the route to well-being and improvement.

I'll continue to take every opportunity to learn when I might be wrong, thus helping to avoid such mistakes in the future.

SEPTEMBER 9

WHAT COMES AROUND

Justice   There's a saying that what goes around, comes around. It's a way of saying that we get back what we give out, and we usually use it to describe a situation in which some particularly villainous person is snared by his or her own schemes.

We can use this same idea as a reminder that our good thoughts and actions also come around to help us as time passes. Whatever effort we put into applying the program and its principles will make an immense difference in our future happiness and well-being. We can go through continuous renewal if we hold fast to the Twelve Step way of life.

We can also know that our work in the program has a role in making the world a better place. Nothing we do along constructive lines is ever lost or wasted if we follow the program.

I'll live today with the knowledge that my Twelve Step program is part of a general movement for peace and well-being in human affairs.

WATCH THOSE FEELINGS

Feelings In AA's early years, there was very little talk about "feelings" or "emotions." The phrase "getting in touch with your feelings" had not been popularized, yet the AA pioneers knew that bitter and resentful feelings were destructive, while warm and optimistic feelings enhanced sobriety.

Now we know that feelings are extremely important for groups as well as individuals. We know that some AA groups can give off feelings that make them more attractive than others. Some groups are considered "cold," while others are "warm." Such differences are rooted in the feelings of each member of the group.

How can we be sure that our feelings will make our groups warm and inviting to others? We can "tune" our feelings by looking at our attitudes. If we are truly dedicated to our principles and want to share them with others, the feelings we project will be welcoming. Whatever we really feel will be expressed in our daily affairs and in our group activities.

I'll check my attitude today for good feelings as I go about my work and activities. These feelings will, in turn, send out signals that everyone can understand and appreciate.

SEPTEMBER 11

WITH WHOM ARE WE HONEST?

Honesty "When you're up before a judge you can't be honest with the court," an AA member said, with some regret. "If you are, the judge will throw the book at you."

This member was right in the sense that courtroom disclosures must always be made with prudence. What's more important is that we are always completely honest with ourselves and the close friends who serve as our sponsors. As for what is disclosed in a court situation, for example, we follow sound professional advice. Under no circumstances, of course, should we tell an outright lie, however.

Our practice of honesty also does not require us to tell every person we know about our alcoholism. We are entitled to our privacy as well as anonymity. Others, in turn, need not be burdened with complete knowledge about our lives.

Our Higher Power will guide us along honest paths once we're committed to the program. We will know when and how to make the right disclosures about ourselves.

I'll practice rigorous honesty today. At the same time, I will be prudent in the way I disclose personal information.

HANDLE THE OLD TAPES WITH CARE

Releasing the Past A large number of recovering people have a tough time coming to terms with the abuse and abandonment of childhood days. Sometimes we play those "old tapes" while reliving the past in a mood of self-pity and resentment. This is destructive.

We cannot completely erase the past, but we can turn it over to our friends and our Higher Power. Our goal should be to transform past experiences into constructive examples.

We can start by reminding ourselves that all unhappy experience is a product of the world's sickness and ignorance. Far from being unusual, our misery was a common thing that we're only now beginning to overcome.

We can also practice God's forgiveness, remembering that real forgiveness is humanly impossible. We should resist the temptation to tell others about our past sufferings in order to gain sympathy. At all times, the old tapes must be handled with care.

Whatever happened in the past cannot affect me today unless I let it. I'll play the old tapes only when it can be done constructively.

LEARNING TO CUT MY LOSSES

Honesty Business people speak of "cutting their losses" when it becomes clear that a venture is going sour. As recovering alcoholics, we need to practice the same principle when we're obviously on the wrong track.

If a resentment is developing, for example, the sooner we spot it and clear it out, the less damage we suffer. In the same way, we may be engaging in selfish but destructive behavior, or perhaps something that borders on being illicit or dishonest. We minimize our losses by admitting the wrong and getting back to our basic principles of living.

In cutting our losses, the usual barriers are pride and self-deception. While these shortcomings will probably always dog us, we at least have experience in dealing with them, or we wouldn't have made any progress in sobriety.

If a course of thought or action isn't working out well, perhaps it's time today to cut my losses in order to get back on the right track.

AM I GETTING TOO BUSY?

Time Management   It's always risky when a recovering person gets too busy for meetings. It's also dangerous when business and personal concerns crowd out interest in the program.

We should never deceive ourselves by thinking that we're somehow safe just because our time is filled with useful and interesting work. Many of us have a tendency to become addicted to "busyness." Though less destructive than drinking, this serves as an escape, just as alcohol did.

The danger is that when the work no longer satisfies us, we'll find our lives becoming empty again. We could then be very vulnerable to taking a drink.

We should never be too busy for the wonderful, constructive work of the program. Far from taking time away from our other activities, work in the program will enhance everything we do.

I'll try to balance my activities today, making sure that I have time for the program.

SEEKING OUR OWN

Harmony Our feelings will often serve as good guides in determining what course of action we ought to follow. If there is a persistent feeling of discomfort about any situation, we should ask ourselves why we are feeling this way. Perhaps it's because we are involved with people or activities that are not right for us.

In the same way, we will feel drawn to certain people and activities. This is undoubtedly because we're in tune with these people or activities.

In such circumstances, we can say that we are "seeking our own." With our unique temperaments and abilities, we fit better in certain places and with certain groups of people than others.

We are indeed fortunate if we find that recovery in a Twelve Step program is a case of seeking and finding our own. This must certainly strengthen and enhance our program.

I'll seek out only the people and activities that seem to belong in my life. If I do not belong in one situation, this merely means that a better one is available somewhere.

SEPTEMBER 16

THE WORLD WILL RECOVER

Belief If our recovery program is working properly, an amazing thing can happen. Instead of being the bad actors of society, we become people who can be considered solid citizens in every way—so square that we might even have sharp corners.

We might then start becoming critical of the world in general. "I've recovered, so why does the rest of the world have to be the way it is?" a person might say. "Why don't other people do something about their resentments and fears, just as I have?"

In asking such a question, we're already in danger of becoming self-righteous. We can remember, however, that our Higher Power has the same concern for others that was shown to us. By the grace of God, and in God's own good time, the world can and will recover.

I'll remember today that God is in charge of the world and will set all things straight, just as I was brought to recovery.

FORMING TRUE PARTNERSHIPS

Intimacy   An early discovery in AA was that alcoholics had trouble forming true partnerships with others. A crippling problem was the real lack of intimacy and honesty in our lives, to say nothing of trust and fairness.

We may continue to have such trouble even in sober living. We may find that many of our friendships are shallow or are based on a single common interest. We think we have close friendships because we play golf or go hunting with certain acquaintances, yet there is no true intimacy in these friendships. Sometimes we even have sexual affairs without really knowing intimacy.

The most common barrier to a true partnership is a mixture of low self-esteem and a fear of having our secrets known. As we put these aside, our partnerships with others will become more satisfactory.

While realizing that none of us can have true partnerships with everyone, I'll strive today to build friendships based on trust and fairness.

THE ROLE OF HUMOR

Attitudes There's a lot of humor among recovery groups, which probably came out of the bizarre drinking stories told by speakers. It's also a reflection of our real personalities.

The right kind of humor helps us achieve balance and not take ourselves too seriously. Meetings can be terribly suffocating when they have neither lightness nor gaiety.

There is also a wrong kind of humor that should be avoided. It's very easy to let joking and good-natured ribbing take the place of the honest discussions all of us need. It's too easy in AA for a member to become known and liked as a charming jokester, even though he or she may be quietly feeling lots of inner pain. People are often surprised when such a person runs into trouble, because they had accepted the humorous surface personality without knowing the real person. In such a case, humor can send the wrong message.

Most of the time, however, humor helps keep us on the right track. Let's keep it in our picture, but also in the proper focus.

I'll not be afraid to laugh at myself or about myself today. Perhaps my right-spirited laughter also reflects the laughter of God.

SEPTEMBER 19

KEEP THE COMMON PROBLEM IN VIEW

Maintaining   If there's been one major change in Alcoholics Anonymous, one old-timer observed, it's probably in group discussions. The focus today is far more on overcoming personal problems than in staying away from the first drink. "The early AA members were continuously concerned about the dangers of drinking," he said. "Members today are more concerned about their feelings and personal issues, such as relationships."

This change has probably been an improvement, but it carries the risk that members will forget why they needed the program in the first place. For alcoholics, it is dangerous to let the problem with alcohol slide out of view. It is important to keep in mind at all times the life-or-death nature of our drinking problem. Even if we are not totally successful in dealing with our feelings or establishing harmonious relationships, it's always necessary to stay sober. Disaster is in that first drink, and let's keep that constantly in view.

No matter how long I've been sober, I'll remind myself several times this day that I'm an alcoholic. I'll also remember that it's only sobriety that enables me to deal with my other problems.

ALL WE NEED TO KNOW

Maintaining Seen from today's perspective, the early AA members had rather narrow attitudes toward the study of alcoholism. They became restless and fidgety if members started discussing psychological aspects of the problem or gave other indications that they were trying to learn more about the disease.

While we don't need to hold such narrow attitudes today, we should at least concede that we don't need complex information to stay sober. All we have to know is that we have a very compulsive problem that can be arrested by eliminating the first drink.

Even today, nobody fully knows why the first drink is so deadly for people like us. Our experience and the experience of others tells us that it is. That knowledge alone can be an important building block in finding and maintaining sobriety.

While being open-minded to new information, I'll remember today that a fairly simple idea—that I'm an alcoholic and can't live with alcohol—is the main thing I need to know.

SEPTEMBER 21

RETURNING TO OLD HAUNTS

Parting with the Past   Recovering alcoholics are usually advised not to return to their old drinking places. If a person is still attracted to such an environment, it's likely that he or she is really entertaining a desire to drink.

We can also "return to our old haunts" by chasing the selfish ways that are more characteristic of drinking than of sober living. Scheming and lying habits, sly extramarital affairs, and other questionable pursuits could be part of the old life that we must leave behind.

Nobody in AA is expected to achieve sainthood or to withdraw from the world. But in living sober, we'll have much greater opportunities for success if we draw a clear line between the old life and the new. There is nothing for us in the old haunts except trouble.

I'll realize today that my new life is different from the old manner of living in many ways. It's much more than just putting the plug in the jug.

MAKING TOUGH DECISIONS

Decision Making   An AA member in a supervisor's position was faced with the need to terminate an unsatisfactory employee. Procrastinating about this unpleasant matter, she found herself wishing that the employee would suddenly find another job, thus making the termination ordeal unnecessary.

But further reflection showed that the procrastination was related to the same problems that had dogged her in her drinking years. She was a people-pleaser; she felt guilty about inflicting pain on others.

She was finally able to make the tough decision and call the employee in for termination. In the process, she discovered that a brief prayer time for preparation and a gentle manner removed some of the pain for her and the employee being terminated. She learned that the principles of the program could help her become more decisive without being brutal.

I'll look over any tough decisions I've been putting off and determine why I'm behaving that way. Am I prolonging tough decisions just as I did when drinking?

WHEN RESENTMENT RETURNS

Inventory   It's surprising and even humiliating to find an old resentment flaring up, sometimes years after we thought it had been put to rest. When that happens, we wonder how thorough we really were in releasing the resentment in the first place.

The secret of handling this problem is to turn the old resentment over to our Higher Power without wasting time wondering why it came up again. We need to deal with it as if it were a brand-new problem; and in a sense, it is.

As for questioning our past sincerity, that too is a waste of time. We are always trying to do our best with the understanding we have for each day. Being too hard on ourselves does not make it easier to practice our program. Resentments can and do return, but they don't have to destroy us.

I'll realize today that I'm always susceptible to any of my ongoing problems, including resentment. Fortunately, I have my program for dealing with them when they occur.

WILLINGNESS TO LISTEN

Willingness Why is it that we'll accept information from some people but not from others? Many people tried to advise us while we were drinking; why would we listen only to recovering alcoholics?

We can't answer that question, except to say that most human beings are willing to listen only to certain people at certain times. That's why business organizations have to select salespeople carefully; customers will respond to some people, but not to others.

As we grow in sobriety, however, we develop the willingness to listen to people we would have once avoided. We can find wonderful ideas in all sorts of places and from all types of people. As we become more open-minded and willing, we can listen more and learn more.

My prejudices and fears of the past kept me from listening to people who would have helped me. I'll be more open-minded and willing today.

A SPIRITED WAY OF LIFE

Spirituality It must be more than coincidence that *spirit* has both high and low meanings for the alcoholic. In its high meaning, *spirit* is the power that rescues us and maintains us in sobriety. In its low meaning, *spirit* is any alcoholic beverage, the route to further destruction.

Carl Jung, whose advice has a link in AA's founding, felt that alcoholics were seeking God, even in their drinking. We were choosing the low spirit because we knew nothing about contacting the high one.

In the Twelve Step program, we learned about contacting a spiritual Power that makes startling and wonderful changes in our lives. People see a new spirit in our lives and a new spirit as we go about our business. This spirited way of life comes from returning to what must be the Source of our being.

I'll remind myself today that the true reality behind everything is Spirit, and this determines the quality of my life.

THE LIMITED AND THE UNLIMITED

Spiritual Growth In our human experience, we face one limitation after another. We are always up against limited time, limited energy, limited knowledge.

Yet everything we're learning tells us that all of these are without limit in the universal. In terms of energy, for example, we know that we would be rich beyond belief if we could really tap the sun's energy that rushes to the earth.

What we call human progress may really refer to the gaining of knowledge that enables us to shake off limitations. We actually did that by becoming sober in our Twelve Step program. Now we're learning to extend our limits in many other ways; and though we are human and limited, we surely have not begun to reach any limits as far as God is concerned. Limited though we seem to be, we're part of a Universe that is without limits.

I'll focus today on the possibility of extending my limits, knowing that this is what God has planned for me.

SEPTEMBER 27

THE TEST OF MY IDEAS

Change   Early in its existence, the AA fellowship tended to resist new ideas, yet did accept many over time. This resistance to new ideas served a good purpose, because it screened out practices that could have destroyed the fellowship.

But other, new ideas have been accepted and have benefited the fellowship. How can we test a new idea before we decide to accept it?

Whatever the idea, it should be beneficial in promoting personal recovery. If it is somehow harmful to those seeking recovery, it should not be accepted.

If this simple test is applied honestly and with fairness, new ideas can be considered on their own merits and can usually be discussed in an atmosphere of reason and understanding. The AA traditions will support most sound ideas.

Knowing that God is the source of new ideas, we can be open to additional guides that can help us along the way. I'll be on the lookout today for any helpful ideas.

THE ROLE OF SELF-SUFFICIENCY

Success When AA was first launched, the ideal of the self-made person was often exalted. Certain outstanding individuals seemed to have achieved amazing success entirely by their own efforts. In the drive to be such a self-made person, AA co-founder Bill W. was swept away in a torrent of alcoholic grandeur.

We know today that there's no such thing as a self-made person. We all need each other, and at various times we would have been lost without assistance that was generously and freely given. Everyone has had such assistance at one time or another. We are not entirely self-sufficient.

The true role of self-sufficiency is to use our talent and opportunities wisely and beneficially in cooperation with others. Our own success in whatever we do will be enhanced as we continue to acknowledge our need for others.

Throughout the day, there will be many times when I need the help of others, and many times when others will need my help. I will give and receive help gratefully.

SEPTEMBER 29

WHEN SHOULD I BE GRATEFUL?

Gratitude   One spiritual writer believed that our only reason for gratitude should be that we are part of God's universe. Others point out that gratitude helps us, not God or the people to whom we are grateful.

Their point is that it's not very uplifting simply to tie our gratitude to certain gifts or benefits. Such gratitude is fairly shallow and is almost no more than good manners. As recovering alcoholics, we need more than that.

The best reason for gratitude is the outlook it creates as we cultivate it within ourselves. We will actually feel mentally and physically uplifted if we know true gratitude. This is the true spiritual outlook alcoholics seek in the bottle but can find only in the new way of life.

I'll find ways to practice gratitude today without letting others know what I'm doing.

HOW DO WE COMMUNICATE?

Carrying the Message   What we are always carries a stronger message than what we say. This is why we're sometimes turned off by people who seek to overwhelm us with charm. It's also why we can sometimes be drawn to people who are quiet and unassuming.

However it works, there is a powerful message in one's unspoken thoughts and feelings. We can usually sense, for example, the mood of people in a room, even when little is being said. If we spend any time with others, they will soon know much about us even if we say little.

This silent communication may be the great secret of AA's success in reaching those who still suffer. If we are living sober and want to help others, that's the message we give out. That's also a form of carrying the message.

I'll communicate today by maintaining a warm and friendly attitude toward every person I meet, knowing that thoughts and feelings speak louder than words.

October

OCTOBER 1

THINKING ABOUT BLAME

Inventory   Which is worse: blaming ourselves or blaming others for things that go wrong? A better question might be, Is anyone to blame?

We're really better off, in Twelve Step living, to begin dropping the idea of placing blame from our thinking altogether. Even if someone's responsibility for a mistake or wrong is fully evident, we get nowhere by pointing the finger at him or her. What often happens, in fact, is that the person becomes defensive—just as we do—and retreats into denial or anger.

Another problem is that placing blame quickly becomes the sticky business of taking another person's inventory. Let's leave such matters to courts and prosecutions and focus instead on solving our own problems.

I'll not waste time today thinking about who's to blame. My focus will be on what can be done for general improvement.

LIVING OR WAITING?

Using Time Wisely What is the real secret of living twenty-four hours at a time? Isn't it really a matter of feeling completely comfortable in the present rather than believing that happiness depends on something in the future?

Whatever our situation today, it's something we must live through and deal with effectively. We may be overlooking many wonderful things in our present life simply because we believe we need some exciting experience that can only come later on.

We also might be overlooking present opportunities because we're spending too much time in the past. The past, whether it was good or bad, is beyond our control.

Our mission is to live effectively and happily today. We can do this best when we realize that yesterday and tomorrow don't really exist—today is all we can be sure of.

I'll live today in the present, handling every problem as well as I can and enjoying every experience that comes to me.

OCTOBER 3

PROVING OURSELVES

Self-Esteem Long after a bitter failure, some of us still cling to the hope that we can erase the defeat in some spectacular way. One dream is to "prove ourselves" to those who scorned us or put us down.

This never really works, even when we do become winners at some later time. For one thing, we may be proving ourselves to people who never will like us. If we are striving to show others that we can succeed, we are still dancing to their tune. We are accepting their idea of what success should be.

Many of us failed simply because we were alcoholics and could do no better. We might have destroyed opportunities that will never arise again. But by finding sobriety, we may already have proved ourselves to those who really count in our lives—including ourselves.

I can prove today that the Twelve Step program works and that a loving Higher Power is present in my life.

DESERVING SUCCESS

Achievements It's said that alcoholics sometimes snatch defeat from the jaws of victory. Some of us, deep down inside, don't really think we deserve success. We might be discouraged by feelings of guilt or low self-esteem, or perhaps we don't want to become targets of envy or competitive attacks.

We need to practice acceptance of our current situation, always believing that we do have a right to achievements that match our talents and experience. Indeed, such achievements may only be possible now that we're sober and thinking rightly.

Some people think that our occupations and our program are separate matters. But the very last idea in the Twelve Steps is to practice our principles "in all our affairs." If we take the view that any useful work is a form of service, we'll find opportunities to be beneficial to everyone. With that attitude, we will also realize that we deserve success.

I'll know today that I have a right to do well in any legitimate activity for which I am qualified.

WHAT CAN SOBRIETY BRING?

Living Sober   The single goal of staying sober is so all-important in AA that side benefits are often overlooked. There is even a tendency to warn members about the hazards of attaching importance to anything except sobriety.

But we do have to become responsible people in all things, not just sober people. We can expect real sobriety to bring the confidence and well-being we expected from the bottle, but never received.

However, we should not expect sobriety to bring us anything that is unrealistic or beyond our capabilities. We will be doing very well if we simply use our own talents in the best way.

Sobriety is not likely to give us the equivalent of the euphoria we got from drinking, but a great sense of well-being based on realistic expectations is more satisfying than the ridiculous mental states we sought in drinking. Living the right kind of life will bring its own rewards.

Along with staying sober today, I'll meet all my responsibilities to my family and friends. Sobriety does not promise miracles, but it does bring a good life.

BY THEIR FRUITS

Inventory An old saying reminds us that the value of any spiritual effort can be measured by how well it works: "A good tree is known by its fruits."

By that standard, the Twelve Step movement fares very well. Its life-changing work has won consistent praise and has had continuous success ever since it became known to the public.

We can apply that same statement to new ideas as they appear in our lives. If somebody has suggestions or advice, we might ask how well such ideas are working out for them. We would not take investment advice, for example, from someone who had repeatedly lost money.

We should always be wary of ideas that go counter to the basic principles of our program. Some people may invite us to share their resentments, for example, but we have no obligation to do so. We will be even less inclined to do so when we look at the results they're getting from their resentments. Evaluating ideas "by their fruits" is a good test.

I'll be careful to look at all the facts in connection with any idea presented today. I have a right to judge everything by results.

TAMING THE INSTINCTS

Orderly Direction   Though alcoholics can appear to have serious shortcomings, these problems are really only misguided attempts to satisfy basic human needs. And we do have instinctive needs that must be met.

In the Twelve Step program, we do not deny our human needs. We realize, however, that these needs must be met in moral, constructive ways. False methods of meeting needs will bring false, harmful results.

We can meet our needs in an orderly manner by turning to our Higher Power and following the Twelve Step principles. This process may seem slow and impractical, but over the longer term we will come to see that it is the right way to live. Our instinctive needs are proper and God-given, but they must not run wild in our lives. Living sober also means taming our instincts.

I'll not be surprised by the various needs I may feel today. I am committed, however, to a moral and principled response to these needs.

CHANGING OTHER PEOPLE

Relating to Others   "How can I get this person to accept the program?" We hear this often, for example, when a patient at a treatment center complains about another who is so negative toward the program "that he's dragging all of us down."

We discovered long ago that we have no power to change or manipulate others. At the very beginning of AA, its pioneers learned how to maintain their own sobriety and serenity even as others rebelled and turned against the program. They learned that negative people can't drag us down unless we let them.

We might need to review our personal inventory if we're too concerned about the behavior of others. Ours is a program of attraction, not coercion, and we "change" people only by demonstrating how well the program works for us. Any concern about another's behavior takes time and energy away from our own commitment to self-improvement.

I have a personal need and responsibility to carry the message, but I have neither the right nor the responsibility to modify anybody's behavior. I'll keep this in mind today.

CAN WE TELL OTHERS
THEY ARE WRONG?

Sharing   As we become more sensitive to others, we soon learn that it's very difficult to tell another person he or she is wrong. Even when we struggle to be kind and diplomatic, we can provoke an angry reaction.

We should not be surprised, because showing people they're wrong is one of the most difficult things in human experience. Few people like to be told that they're wrong, as we can see when our wrongs are advertised to others.

There is almost no way to directly tell people they're wrong without hurting or offending them. Furthermore, if they are hurt or offended, they might fell less inclined to work to correct their behavior.

If we've taken the Twelve Step principles to heart, however, we learn first that we are usually not required to tell anybody that he or she is wrong. But we *can* help people simply by relating accounts of situations when we were wrong and what we did to change. If done properly, this gives the other person the opportunity to change without feeling resentment or humiliation.

I'll try to be as sensitive as possible to the feelings of others. I'll be especially careful about trying to show them that they're wrong.

PUTTING OUR TRUST IN PEOPLE

Trust   How much should we trust other people? This is an important question, because many of us have erred in both directions; we've trusted people too much or not enough.

We can find our answer in the spiritual side of the program. We do have a Higher Power in whom we can have absolute trust. We can have little doubt that the spiritual presence behind everything is infallible and supreme.

As human beings, we know that we can only be trusted in certain ways. We can work to develop our trustworthiness, but it is never high enough, even with the strongest souls. All of us have weaknesses that can keep us from being what we know to be our best.

In our Twelve Step living, we should work to develop trust in both ourselves and others, but not be hurt or disappointed when things go wrong. Above all, our real trust should be in our Higher Power.

I'll work today to be trusting and trustworthy, but I'll not expect too much of anybody, including myself.

OCTOBER 11

KEEPING ANGER IN SAFE LIMITS

Dealing with Anger "The most heated bit of letter-writing can be a wonderful safety valve," AA cofounder Bill W. said, "providing the wastebasket is somewhere nearby."

This is a delightful bit of advice about the right way to handle anger. Writing an angry letter is at least a way of bringing our feelings out so that we can see them. This is far healthier than the peculiar method of "stuffing" one's feelings and pretending that there was no hurt or offense.

But an angry letter, once mailed, can be more destructive than a bullet. We may live to regret ever having mailed it. It could have unintended consequences of the worst kind.

That's why the wastebasket becomes the second handy way to deal with our anger. We throw the letter away and let time and wisdom heal the matter. What usually happens under the guidance of our Higher Power is that we find a much more satisfactory way of settling whatever has happened.

If I become angry today, I'll admit it to myself. Perhaps I'll even put my feelings on paper. But I'll have the good sense not to go further with such outbursts.

A FATAL FEATURE OF ALCOHOLISM

Admitting Defeat Part of alcoholism's deadliness lies in its peculiar tendency to blind the victim to the hopelessness of the situation. Time and again, AA members meet people who are in the final stages of their disease, yet are still clinging to the fallacy that things are not as bad as they seem. Indeed, many alcoholics who have engineered their own ruin still believe they were either victims of bad luck or of malevolent action by others.

Those of us who recover can be grateful that we were brought to understand that we were without hope until we found help in the program. This was our lifeline to a safe recovery.

Let's remember, however, that others might not be so fortunate. We must not criticize them for not being able to accept the hopelessness of their condition. We should also look for our own blind spots about other problems in our lives.

I'll remember today that only the Twelve Step program arrested my fatal disease and keeps it at bay. I'll feel kindly toward others who are having trouble admitting defeat; maybe this is the day it will happen for them.

WHEN ARE WE RECEIVING GUIDANCE?

Guidance We have to face the fact that what we see as divine guidance may simply be an expression of self-will. We are all too familiar with examples of people who did terrible things, claiming to be obeying orders from God.

We cannot judge whether another is really receiving guidance from a Higher Power. In our own lives, however, we can learn to distinguish between God's guidance and our self-will. The outstanding characteristic of a divinely guided action is the strong sense of peace it brings. Even if we have to deny ourselves for a time, we sense that the final outcome of any decision will be beneficial for all concerned. We do not have to argue for or defend our decision.

When self-will is in the saddle, we may find ourselves being called on to justify our actions. We may also have to quell or rationalize feelings of guilt or doubt.

The right answers come when self-will is working in harmony with the Higher Will. Our lives will have a quality that everybody senses, including ourselves.

Knowing that self-will can easily lead me astray, I'll listen today for the divine voice of my Higher Power

WHAT IS TRUE SHARING?

Sharing Though it comes without a price, the sharing we undertake in the AA program has value without limits. When we share our experience, strength, and hope with others, we become both teachers and friends.

Sometimes we are led to believe that we should share our material goods with others, but all we learn is that this often fails to help anyone. Such sharing is not wrong, but it can be misused and misdirected.

In the form of sharing we practice in AA, there can be only gain for all involved in the exchange. Our sharing of personal experience may be just what another person needs at the time. What also matters is that we need it and can benefit from it.

True sharing of this kind is one of the great secrets of AA's success. If our program isn't working well, perhaps we should do more of this sharing.

I'll seek to share my true feelings with others today, in the hope that this will help all of us.

READING ABOUT OURSELVES

Gratitude It's not only the experiences of our fellow AA members that can help us in recovery. We should also be able to see ourselves in stories about troubled people in the grip of alcoholism and anger.

Quite often, if we're truly honest, we can even see ourselves in tragic accounts of alcoholics who harmed others during drunken rages or blackouts. We might have stopped short of such behavior, but could this have happened to us? We might read of a drunken driving accident, for example, and realize that we narrowly escaped one or might have caused one had we not found sobriety.

Reading such accounts gives us deep pity and sympathy for all the people involved. These stories make us realize that alcoholism has many victims in addition to those who are afflicted with the disease. And we should be grateful that sobriety enabled some of us to stay out of such news stories and not add to the world's problems.

Whatever happens today, I'll at least be grateful that sobriety can keep me from causing the out-of-control situations I read about in the daily newspapers.

OCTOBER 16

HOMELESS AND UNEMPLOYED

Economic Insecurity   Alcoholism isn't the sole cause of the homelessness and unemployment that troubles our world. Even in sobriety, people can lose their jobs and homes, through no fault of their own.

Recovery makes it less likely that we will cause such conditions in our own lives. Beyond that, by keeping sober, we will be better able to deal with any setbacks that do occur. It is a painful fact that it is almost impossible to help any destitute alcoholic find a home or employment unless he or she stops drinking. We learn that much through our experience.

Our true home is with our Higher Power, and our best work may be in the sharing of our experience and strength with others. Remembering this, we can be sympathetic and understanding about the general problems of homelessness and unemployment. We don't have the complete answer, but we do have answers.

I'll be grateful and understanding in any consideration of today's problems of homelessness and unemployment. By staying sober, I am at least helping to alleviate some of the general problems.

DRIVEN BY FEAR

Finding Courage   During any group discussion of fear, someone usually points out that it serves a protective purpose by keeping us out of harm's way.

With the types of fear that drove us, however, we more often fled into further harm while trying to avoid the threats at hand. No person whose fear reaches a panic stage can effectively control his or her actions.

We cannot expect sobriety alone to make us exempt from fear. What it can do is give us an ability to handle our fear constructively.

There are steps to doing this. First, we should not be too prideful to admit that fear can come to us. Second, we should admit it when we do feel fear. Third, we can discuss our fear with others while turning it over to our Higher Power.

It would be wonderful if these steps then lifted us above any sense of fear. Even if this doesn't happen completely, we've succeeded in mastering our problem if we don't let fear drive us to work against ourselves. If I am afraid to give a presentation for work or go for a job interview, for example, I am being driven into inaction. This must not be allowed to happen.

I can find courage today in the Twelve Step program. This will enable me to act properly and responsibly, even if I'm a bit queasy with fear.

THOSE WHO WANT IT,
NOT THOSE WHO NEED IT

Honest Desire In the first bloom of sobriety, many recovering people confront drinking companions who also "need" the program. They're often surprised and disillusioned when efforts to help their friends are rejected—sometimes curtly.

We're truly limited to helping those who desire recovery, not those who we think need it. Though intervention methods can be effective, we're still largely helpless to assist those who don't desire recovery.

We regret that we really have no answers for the millions who perish from alcoholism, unaware of their problem. We also can hold out little hope that any future recovery attempts will succeed without the individual alcoholic's cooperation.

Desire—a personal determination and decision—is necessary for almost any kind of change. We have the freedom to choose in many areas of our lives, and alcoholics must eventually choose recovery in order to find and maintain it.

Though I'd love to see others recover, I must accept the fact that their personal desire and choice is necessary. I'll remember this if any opportunities arise today to carry the message.

THE SAME SITUATION—
OVER AND OVER

Growth in Maturity Our drinking experience should have taught us that we'll continue to repeat old destructive behaviors until we change our attitudes.

In sobriety, we can take this idea a step further and apply it to other areas. If we have trouble with other people, for example, we should ask what we're doing to bring about unpleasant situations.

This is not to say that we're responsible for everything that goes wrong, but we are getting a message about ourselves if we continuously meet the same problem in different forms. Some people, for example, repeatedly become involved in bad relationships or find themselves working for abusive bosses.

Just as a changed attitude helped us recover from our drinking problem, so can a new attitude keep us from repeating other destructive situations.

I'll be on the lookout today for any indication of a tendency to "attract" trouble. It's true that I can have bad luck, but I don't need to bring it on myself.

THIS TOO SHALL PASS

Acceptance   When personal problems are brought up in group discussions, someone usually remembers the saying, "This too shall pass." We use it in reference to unpleasant matters, but it also applies to happier experiences. It is a certainty that nothing will ever stay the same.

Our responsibility to ourselves is to see all situations constructively, whether they are seen as good or bad at the time. What seems a disappointment today might be seen as a blessing tomorrow. And we can't always be sure that today's wonderful opportunity doesn't have a few hidden nettles in it.

The one certainty is that everything will pass. We should extract the good from everything, and let what is unpleasant fade into the past.

Whatever I'm facing today will certainly change as I do my best in the twenty-four hours ahead. None of us is permanently bound to any problem.

OCTOBER 21

HOW DO WE HELP OTHERS?

Carrying the Message   We may be disillusioned by the selfish behavior we see around us, but many people and groups do dedicate themselves to helping others. Sometimes, however, even their efforts fail, or are misunderstood and even resented.

In AA, we don't have solutions for every human problem—though some believe our program is widely applicable. But we can help people in a surprising and simple way by showing how well the program works in our own lives.

This provides role models of recovery for others who struggle in the bondage of alcoholism. We are giving them convincing evidence that the program does work.

We also help by sharing how our recoveries came about and how we maintained our sobriety. This is a form of helping that benefits everyone. Furthermore, we can be assured that we will be helped, even when our efforts to help others don't seem to be succeeding.

I'll expect to help somebody today, preferably by carrying the message of recovery. One person is certain to benefit from this.

WHEN THE BATH IS NEGATIVE

Personal Relations   A member referred to getting a "negative bath" every day at work. She was talking about her boss's bad disposition and the poor attitudes of several co-workers. How does one deal with this negativity?

It's not satisfactory to say that this member created her own "negative bath" by her attitudes toward her boss and others. In fact, in many businesses, the atmosphere *is* negative—and dealing with it takes more than trite comment.

In such situations, we can employ detachment, as practiced in Al-Anon, and accept the things we cannot change, as stated in the Serenity Prayer.

The longer-term solution may require making a major change, such as finding a new job, but we must be careful not to exchange one negative situation for another. We will make the right decision if we're careful to avoid resentment and self-pity while being completely honest about our own motives and intentions.

I may find myself in a "negative bath" of some kind today, but I can detach from it by avoiding resentment or the tendency to blame others.

HOW DO WE HURT OTHERS?

Inventory Even while drinking, few of us abused others physically or committed crimes. Yet we did harm others, even when we thought we were hurting only ourselves.

One way we harmed others—and this applies to many alcoholic family relationships—was by withholding the love and support they needed. If we had a nasty disposition at times, this poisoned the atmosphere and made others uncomfortable and afraid.

Maybe we harmed others by not being productive at work. Our absenteeism, for example, may have put our boss in a bad light with superiors or caused the firm to lose a client.

Perhaps the worst harm was in being completely indifferent to what we were doing to others. Any willingness to admit wrong, then, can be a major step toward recovery and self-improvement.

Though I have no intention of harming anyone today, I'll realize that even my attitude can affect others unfavorably. I'll try to maintain an attitude that's uplifting to everyone.

LIGHT FOR DARK CORNERS

Honesty Newspaper writers know that there's usually a future story in the "dark side" of any person who is being lavishly praised in the media. That's because almost every person has a "dark side," or secrets that are carefully guarded.

We should look for such dark corners in our own lives. Most of us are not public figures fearing exposure, but recovering people seeking to stay sober and healthy.

We can begin to illuminate our dark corners by discussing our secrets with others. This does not necessarily eliminate whatever shortcoming is involved, but our honesty is a step in the right direction.

False pride may also play a part in keeping dark secrets from others, causing fear that others might see us as we really are. Thus, learning to confront and confess our dark sides can lead to victory over both fear and pride.

I'll strive today to be honest about any weaknesses or wrongs that I've been concealing. Under the light of such honesty, my dark secrets can be transformed.

DIFFERENT ROUTES TO ALCOHOLISM

Understanding Powerlessness   While alcoholics have much in common, the personal stories heard at AA open meetings show that we took different routes to alcoholism. Some became out-of-control drinkers almost from the beginning. Others lost control slowly after years of seemingly moderate drinking.

These difference are underscored by the fact that we also differ in physical and emotional traits. Some alcoholics, for example, were so emotionally disturbed that they became problem drinkers from the very start. Some appeared to "have it all together," yet became alcoholics after retirement or some other change in life patterns.

Whatever the route taken, we share in common our individual powerlessness at the time we knocked on AA's door. And the solution for each of us was the same: sobriety in AA.

The risk in listening to such different personal accounts is that some of us twist these differences into "proof" that we are not alcoholics. The reward of such sharing, however, is learning that we do have a common problem and that there is a solution that fits everyone, in spite of our differences.

I'll remember today that I came to AA because I was powerless over alcohol. That has not changed.

WHO IS AN ALCOHOLIC?

AA's Mission Though AA's avowed mission is to carry its message to alcoholics, the fellowship does not really have a one-size-fits-all definition of alcoholism. This has created some confusion when nonalcoholics inadvertently show up at meetings that are supposed to be for alcoholics only, or when people with other addictions seek AA's help. A few groups even insist that people must declare themselves alcoholics in order to participate in a "closed" meeting.

But who *is* an alcoholic? The AA pioneers were not insistent that people should immediately declare themselves alcoholics in order to receive help. Newcomers were invited to attend meetings and then decide for themselves if they were alcoholics and needed the program. In today's environment, we have the added factor that troubled people might be addicted to both drugs and alcohol. Such cross-addiction, in fact, seems to be a strong trend. We also know that any alcoholic can easily become cross-addicted if he or she uses other drugs.

Our best course is to keep the door open for any person who comes to AA sincerely desiring help. If people find their answers in AA, they probably belong in the fellowship.

I'll be grateful today that I was able to admit that I had a problem and needed AA's help. I'll accept others just as I was accepted. To stay sober and grow in the program, I do not need to define alcoholism for anybody other than myself.

IS YOUR OPINION OF ME IMPORTANT?

Inventory   A statement that is often quoted at AA meetings is "Your opinion of me is not important." The purpose of this saying, apparently, is to wean us away from being "people-pleasers."

But the truth is that we all have legitimate interest in the opinions others hold of us. They may like or dislike us for all the wrong reasons, but it is helpful for us to know this and accept it.

More important, the opinions of others can be useful in helping us take personal inventory and correct wrong behavior and attitudes. There may be a good reason why someone has a low opinion of us, and we should become aware of it.

It is true, however, that *our* opinions count the most in shaping our lives. If we're thinking badly about others, that can be more damaging to us than to them. Surprisingly, they may think better of us as we change our opinions about them.

I doubt that I can go through the day without being affected by other people's opinions of me. However, my main work will be in seeing that my own opinions aren't being destructive in my life.

THE NEW PROBLEMS IN SOBRIETY

Fortitude Sometimes sobriety turns up problems that were never apparent during one's drinking days. Some people, for example, encounter marriage problems that lead to divorce. It almost appears that some things were better when we were drinking.

But there are good reasons why sobriety brings new problems. One is that we become aware of problems that were there all the time, although not acknowledged. It's possible, too, that sobriety brings more responsibility, along with risks of failure. At the same time, we might be more sensitive to the real problems of living.

We should never use such problems as an excuse for drinking. It is true, as many people say, that drinking can only make matters worse. Nothing can be improved by a return to drinking.

I must remember today that sobriety means living on a new basis. This includes facing problems and dealing with them—not running from them as I did in the past.

DIMINISHING RETURNS
ARE STILL BENEFICIAL

Getting Better   There's a "Cloud Nine" effect that some of us had when we first found sobriety. Some call it the honeymoon stage. It includes a feeling of great joy and relief over having found, at last, an answer to drinking.

This gradually fades away, as it should under normal conditions. We then feel as though we're in stages of diminishing returns, where the benefits don't seem as miraculous, and other improvements in our lives seem to come slowly.

The experience we have in getting sober is like that of people who recover from a terrible physical illness. At first, they feel remarkably better for the first time. But then their recovery becomes taken for granted, and "feeling better" isn't as remarkable as it was when they first recovered.

We should not expect it to be. Instead, we can focus on the contentment and well-being that living sober and steady improvement give us.

I may not have anything today like the excitement that accompanied early recovery. I'll be satisfied with the normal blessings of good living.

OCTOBER 30

WHO IS A WINNER?

Staying Sober Newcomers in AA are urged to "stick with the winners." But who is a winner?

A winner in AA is one who finds sobriety and represents principles that help others find and maintain sobriety. Any person who can help others is a winner.

The losers are people who don't make enough of a commitment to find and maintain sobriety. It may not be their fault. On the other hand, some losers eventually become winners.

It is not our purpose to apply ratings to various individuals, whether they're winner or losers. We must know, however, that we cannot benefit from the suggestions of people who do not stay sober. We are looking for the path of recovery, not the road to ruin. The winners are people who can help us in our recovery.

I'll spend as much time as possible with people who want to stay sober. I have no intention of joining anyone on the road to ruin.

OCTOBER 31

BE STILL—
FOR A WHILE, ANYHOW

God's Will for Us   The Bible reminds us: "Be still, and know that I am God." What does this say to the recovering alcoholic who is struggling against a tidal wave of problems?

It must be a reminder that our true place and right work is part of a great purpose, though we may still not know how we fit into the larger plan. We can know, however, that God's plan will include peaceful actions, just and moral solutions, and results that are wholly beneficial to all concerned.

One does not have to be a theologian to decide that staying sober is part of God's will for us. That's why we can expect the support of Higher Power at all times, even when we feel fearful and abused.

Aside from staying sober, each of us will have individual work and responsibilities in life. We should be careful not to measure anyone's success—including our own—against worldly standards. If God is in charge, wherever we are and whatever we happen to be doing can be a part of the divine will.

In keeping sober today, I'll know that I'm carrying out God's will. I'll also be open to unexpected opportunities to carry out God's directions.

November

NOVEMBER 1

DO WE HAVE FREE WILL?

Free Choice The question of a human being's free will has been argued for centuries by learned individuals. We can answer it for ourselves as a result of our experience in AA.

Our freedom was lost while we were in the grip of alcohol. Once free of drink, we still realized that many things in life are controlled by other people and things, such as political and economic forces.

If our employer closes the business, for example, we may have to choose less satisfactory employment. If a person threatens physical violence, we may have to go along with his or her wishes against our will.

In all circumstances, our free will lies in the way we choose to think about what's happening. We always have the choice of turning to our Higher Power in thought, rather than reacting with fear and resentment. This is the only free will we can possibly have in the world, but it may be all we really need.

If a difficult situation or problem arises, I'll remember that no human power could have relieved my alcoholism. This will remind me that the true source of power is always at hand.

NOVEMBER 2

GOD'S WILL AND MY WILL

False Gods? It is always risky to announce with certainty what we believe God's will to be, even for ourselves. It is rarely helpful to use one's material success as an example of God's grace. "Isn't God a millionaire?" a spiritual leader was quoted as saying in defense of his luxurious lifestyle.

It is reasonable to believe that God will guide us to the right career and business opportunities that fit our needs. We can even believe that universal prosperity is part of God's plan, though we're far short of it now. We need not envy wealthy people, nor should we want to take what they have.

The real danger of equating prosperity with God's will is that the material quickly becomes dominant. We might also fall into the trap of gauging spiritual progress by our bank balance. This can lead to selfishness and arrogance, which immediately drive out spiritual power. We already had the bitter experience of making a false god out of alcohol. We must not make new false gods out of material success.

I'll accept any material success with gratitude, knowing that my real trust must be in God.

LIVING WITH IMPOSSIBLE DREAMS

Hope and False Hope No matter how badly we managed our lives while drinking, many of us survived by holding on to the hope that some great stroke of luck would rescue us. Either we would find a windfall to pay off our debts, or a kind benefactor would appear to set things right.

These were impossible dreams, but they helped sustain us in the miserable half-world of alcoholism. We could not see that drinking was the real problem.

But we did have our great stroke of luck in finding AA. This helped us face our debts. At the same time, we found benefactors in the form of sponsors and other friends. We also found a Higher Power.

Even in sobriety, we have to guard against the impossible dreams we nourished while drinking. Again and again, we must remind ourselves that sober living is based on reality. Even reality, however, can have its miracles.

I'll keep my dreams alive today, but I'll make sure that they have a good foundation in reality.

THE GIFT OF SENSITIVITY

Facing Reality   Some of us complain about being too sensitive, or others may tell us so. This sets us up for all kinds of hurts, both real and imaginary.

In drinking, we actually dulled our sensitivity, though we thought we were expressing more feelings. This dulling of our sensitive nature blinded us to the damage we were doing.

In sobriety, we are learning that sensitivity is a gift that we can channel wisely. It can make us more aware of the feelings and needs of others. It can help us become a part of the group.

Like all gifts, sensitivity has its downside. It can make us vulnerable to problems that do not belong to us, and it can lead us into the trap of worrying about things we can do nothing about. But sensitivity is generally good, and in sobriety we can become better people because of it.

I'll take great satisfaction today in the full use of my senses, including that part of me that perceives and expresses deep feelings.

NO APOLOGIES FOR SOBRIETY

Attitude Now that we are sober, some of us are invited to social events where there is drinking. Now and then, we see raised eyebrows when others learn that we're having only soft drinks.

Some of us may respond by explaining that we're alcoholics and cannot take even one drink. A few recovering alcoholics handle the situation by pretending that they're holding an alcoholic drink—perhaps enlisting the bartender's aid in making the drink appear to contain liquor.

While it may be useful to tell others about our alcoholism, we are under no obligation to do so, particularly in a drinking environment. At the same time, there's something wrong with pretending that one is still taking alcoholic drinks.

Our best course is to remember that we never have to apologize for not drinking. In a world that makes so much fuss about the right to drink, we surely have a right not to drink, and we do not have to explain why we are not drinking.

If I find myself in a drinking environment today, I'll handle it with dignity and cheerfulness, but I will not feel that I must defend my sobriety to others.

NOVEMBER 6

DEALING WITH WORRY

Dealing with Feelings There's nothing like a siege of worry to spoil our day. It matters little whether the worry is about a real problem or something we're imagining. In either case, worry makes us unhappy, depressed, and even fatigued.

It doesn't help to be urged not to worry. We may even know worry is harmful, yet be unable to stop it. In fact, one of the things we may have sought in the bottle was an easing of worry.

The best answer to worry is in the Twelve Step program. If we have turned our will and lives over to our Higher Power, the real direction of our lives is out of our hands. We must think of ourselves as passengers in a divinely guided vehicle.

Some will think this philosophy is preposterous and irresponsible, but in reality we are taking right actions in an orderly way, as our guidance continues. We need only prove to ourselves that our program works. Worry is merely a signal that we need to work our program.

If I catch myself worrying, I'll remind myself that my Higher Power is in charge of all outcomes. I'll do my best and expect the best.

NOVEMBER 7

SINCERITY AT THE BEGINNING

Self-Honesty   We were told at our first AA meeting that half-measures will avail us nothing. What's needed is a sincere desire to stop drinking and seek a new way of life.

As we continue in the program, we learn that sincerity is an ingredient for success in everything we do. Quite often, we may find that we're failing in something simply because our heart isn't really in it.

We can't force ourselves into a sincere posture. Instead, the answer is to know ourselves well enough to know just how we feel about everything we do.

We'll learn to be careful about attempting to do something when our heart is not really in it. We may be doing something we dislike merely for the recognition and money it gives us. For real sincerity, we need more than that, and the truths of the program will help us find it.

I'll be conscious today of the sincerity I have about the things I am attempting to do. There may be some things I need to abandon or at least change.

NOVEMBER 8

PROVING GOD'S EXISTENCE

Belief   It surprised some of us to learn that the AA Big Book has a chapter about agnosticism. The agnostic is one who believes the existence of God cannot be proved; and indeed, some of us liked to explain this during profound barroom discussions.

Our experience with a Higher Power does not really settle the questions about God or the purpose and meaning of life. We may still wonder why we are on Earth and what the universal system is all about.

We can prove, however, that our lives can become dramatically different as a result of our belief in God. While some people scoff that our belief in a Higher Power is merely psychological, we will know that it is far more than that. This belief seems to be something that we need just as we require physical nourishment.

It's not necessary to join the debating society that seeks to prove or deny God's existence. For our purposes, it's only necessary to believe that God exists in our lives.

I'll not concern myself with any general question about the existence or nonexistence of God. What's important is to know that my Higher Power is living and working in my sphere of activities.

NOVEMBER 9

COMPLIANCE ISN'T ACCEPTANCE

Honesty We are sometimes mystified when people come into the AA program, respond to its message for months or years, and then disappear, seemingly without a trace. Later, we may be shocked to learn that they're drinking again.

While we have no way of knowing the real reason, one possible explanation is that they were practicing compliance without really accepting the program. The danger of compliance is that it may simply be an outward show of working the program while leaving one's real thoughts and feelings unchanged.

At the same time, we often urge people to practice what is really only a form of compliance. We tell them, for example, to "bring the body" to meetings in the belief that the heart will follow. This does little good if one's heart does not follow!

The only solution is to continue the difficult but rewarding search for honesty in all things. When we examine ourselves honestly, we will recognize when we are truly accepting and when we are merely complying.

I'll remember today that the real success of AA is not in the number of people who show up at meetings, but in how we truly accept the program.

HONESTY WITH ANOTHER PERSON

Admitting Wrongs A good Fifth Step in the program means being entirely honest with at least one person about the nature of our shortcomings. "A burden shared is a burden cut in half" is the principle behind this action.

We can feel relieved that the Twelve Step program specifically limits this sharing to "another person"—though we can obviously add to that if we choose. However, we must be sure to share honestly with that one person, being careful not to gloss over this important Step.

What is the result of this honest sharing? At the very least, it helps us lose the fear that people might know us as we really are. It helps us face the world with confidence and perhaps new humility. Moreover, it can strengthen our ability to stay sober. All these gains are certainly reward enough.

If I haven't been honest with at least one other person, I'll reread the Fifth Step today. This is something that should be done for my own future safety and well-being.

NOVEMBER 11

THE REWARDS OF TRUTH

Seeking the Truth "The punishment of the liar is that he cannot believe anyone else," wrote one shrewd philosopher. This is another way of saying that we reap what we sow, or that we tend to judge others by our own actions.

But when we decide to be completely truthful, we are not immediately given the ability to discern whether others are lying or not. It's more important for us to realize that others' lies don't have the power to hurt us permanently if we persevere in the program.

Some people would argue with this, pointing to lies that have hurt innocent people in the past. But having no way of knowing all the facts of these cases, we cannot be the judge.

In our own experience, we'll find that God alone is the source of all truth and will give us the protection and care we need if we seek truthfulness in everything we do. Any fear of being victimized by lying, we'll learn, will melt away as we follow this conviction.

I'll be as discreet as possible today, but I'll also be truthful. I'll find that this alone will lessen any fear of being victimized by a liar.

NOVEMBER 12

THE IMPORTANCE OF MAINTENANCE

Fortitude In praising their success with AA, people sometimes overlook the importance of maintenance. AA not only helps us achieve sobriety, but it can also help us maintain our sobriety for a lifetime.

Members often touch on this matter when they admit that they were able to sober up hundreds of times, but didn't know how to *stay* sober. It is staying sober that makes all the difference between life and death for us.

Our tools for staying sober—for maintaining our sobriety—are the simple ones that put us back on our feet in the first place. We continue to admit that we're alcoholics and need the help of fellow members and our Higher Power. We also continue to attend meetings and to carry the message. We remind ourselves that we're never out of the woods permanently, no matter how much our lives improve.

I'll take the routine steps today that are needed for the maintenance of my sobriety. Doing this will help protect me from the terrible consequences of returning to drinking.

NOVEMBER 13

THE BOREDOM BATTLE

Acceptance and Patience All of us have times when we don't enjoy our sobriety as much as we feel we should. Though we're still grateful, we sometimes feel bored and depressed.

What we have to remember at such times is our bleak history of using alcohol as a quick fix for boredom. However ruinous and false it proved to be, alcohol did temporarily bring the miraculous change we sought.

We thought of alcohol as a means of uplifting our mood. We were very surprised to learn that it's really a depressant. Maybe it lifted us up by depressing our self-doubt and self-criticism.

Whatever the nature of our drinking, we need to stay sober while fighting our battles with boredom. We can do that by accepting a bit of boredom without succumbing to it. Meanwhile, we can look for ways of easing boredom that don't get us into trouble or lead back to the bottle.

I'll not feel guilty or unworthy if boredom strikes me now and then. Today I'll help manage my long-term boredom tendencies by practicing acceptance and patience for twenty-four hours.

NOVEMBER 14

NO RESPECTER OF PEOPLE

Carrying the Message   As human beings, we have to realize that some people are more attractive to us than others. Even in AA, we will likely be more interested in a person who has qualities we admire than one who annoys and repels us.

This is a snobbish attitude that we ridicule when we see it practiced by others, but we may be practicing it in our own way by seeking out only those members we find interesting and attractive. Without realizing it, we can be making AA a popularity contest, which it's not supposed to be.

We can compensate for such tendencies by making a special effort to express friendship to everyone at the meeting. This can even become a spiritual exercise. It doesn't hurt to admit that one has snobbish tendencies that can violate the spirit of AA.

Just as alcohol is no respecter of people, so it is that the program should be open to all. Today, I'll try to make AA a welcoming haven for everyone.

THE LOSS OF CHOICE

Freedom   Many alcoholics are vigorous defenders of free choice. We have to concede, however, that our choices are not always limited by the tyranny of others. Our own actions can take away our freedom of choice.

Recovering people in AA have learned that taking even one drink will result in the loss of choice, and it is not just a temporary loss of sobriety that one faces. It's always possible that the person who drinks again may never recover sobriety.

In the same way, other actions represent loss of choice in our lives. A person who cheats, for example, may learn that he or she has no choice over the unpleasant outcomes that follow.

We can protect our freedom of choice by deciding only to take actions that will strengthen such freedom in the future. At no time should we make any choices that rob us of our precious right to choose.

Every action I take today must help me keep favorable options open in the future. My right to choose was restored by AA, and I must help protect it.

NOVEMBER 16

KEEPING SOBRIETY ROLLING

Continuing to Follow A child learning to ride a bicycle discovers that it only takes gentle pedaling to keep the bike in motion. The more difficult task was getting on the bike and maintaining a straight course in the right direction.

Staying sober in AA seems to be the same kind of thing. It may take a lot of effort and self-honesty to establish sobriety, but a routine of simple steps can keep it going on a daily basis. For most people, daily meditations and regular attendance at meetings are enough to maintain a straight course in the right direction.

The danger comes when people become too lazy or careless to take even these simple steps. Then, like a bike losing forward momentum, they can wobble and fall.

Even at the point of wobbling, one can get a bike up to speed again and gain stability. This is something to remember if we find our own sobriety becoming wobbly.

Nothing can be so important today that it keeps me from doing the simple things needed for continuous sobriety. I'll remember the bike.

NOVEMBER 17

ARE WE DOING WELL ENOUGH?

Success Sometimes we can get off the track by mixing AA with the world's ideas of success.

In AA, success means staying sober while using the AA principles in our daily affairs. We can be successful people in all walks of life.

We should never think that a person is unsuccessful merely because he or she holds a low-paying job or has not regained any business or professional stature that has been lost. One of our members, for example, had once been the senior member of a lucrative law partnership before drinking himself into the gutter. In his sober years, he found great satisfaction in a relatively low-paying judgeship. In worldly terms, he could be seen as less successful. In AA terms, however, this period was the truly successful part of his life.

Our Higher Power will show us where our place in life should be. That should be success enough for any of us.

I'll do my very best today in whatever job I have, grateful for the sobriety that helps me stay self-supporting and happy.

NOVEMBER 18

THE OLD FRIENDS WHO DROPPED US

Personal Relations   As our drinking progressed, most of us lost old friends. Sometimes it was our behavior that drove them away; at other times, it was because they didn't want to associate with "losers."

In sobriety, some of our old friendships have been restored. These are the real friendships based on trust and true affection.

But sobriety can also give us a deeper and finer understanding of friendships. We may acquire a new set of values on this subject. We may find that some of those whom we considered friends were only fair-weather drinking acquaintances.

Drinking acquaintances will probably ease away from us if we really mean business in staying sober. This need not bother us if we're thinking rightly.

The great news in all of this is that in the fellowship, we'll be making some of the best friends we can ever have. We'll also learn how to be great friends with ourselves.

In my thinking about friendship today, I'll seek people I trust and like, not people I can use.

NOVEMBER 19

IS THERE BONDAGE
IN ATTENDING MEETINGS?

Sharing A few critics have noted scornfully that AA members can be as enslaved by the need for meetings as we were by the bottle. Are we compulsively addicted to meetings?

When we hear such remarks, we must remember that our survival in sobriety is always the main issue. We might be going to more meetings than seems necessary, but we are the judges of our own needs.

In addition, meeting attendance is a constructive activity, while drinking was destructive—at least for us. If we're going to overdo something, at least it's an activity that helps us.

We should never consider meeting attendance a form of bondage. There are many activities in life that are required for our peace and freedom. Meeting attendance is one of these things. We can be grateful for the opportunities meetings provide for sharing our personal experiences. No criticism should be allowed to intrude on this.

I'll not let outside criticism interfere with any AA activity that is benefiting me and maintaining my sobriety.

NOVEMBER 20

ESTRANGEMENTS

Amends A number of alcoholics become estranged from members of their family. Sometimes these estrangements continue into sobriety and fester as a source of resentment.

Where estrangements have occurred, we are always responsible for any wrongs on our part. We need to check carefully to make sure that pride and bitterness on our part aren't prolonging the estrangement.

But some of these estrangements have been chosen by others. We need to accept them if we've done everything possible to correct the problem.

Honesty will be our guide as we look carefully at any estrangements in our lives. All that's ever necessary is that we use our best principles in dealing with any estrangements.

If I find today that an estrangement is bothering me or others in the program, I'll examine it carefully with the thought that either making amends or acceptance might be required.

ALCOHOLISM IN THE WORKPLACE

Employment   Most of the personal stories in AA include troubles in the workplace. This is not surprising, because the disease itself almost guarantees that an active alcoholic is likely to make more mistakes, have higher absenteeism, and get into trouble with bosses and/or fellow employees. Who really wants a *practicing* alcoholic on the payroll? Who would want such a person as a manager or employer? Who wants to be treated by a doctor who is drunk or badly hung over?

If our alcoholism created problems in the workplace, we have no moral right to blame others who held us accountable for this. Far from blaming others who were critical of us, we owe personal amends for any harm we caused employers or fellow workers.

The good news is that recovery makes it possible for us to perform up to acceptable standards at work and carry out our responsibilities. In sobriety, we can write a new chapter and establish a good work history.

In my work today, I'll keep in mind the wonderful advantages I have as a result of knowing and practicing the AA principles. As a recovering alcoholic, I can be a positive force in an organization.

TOO SMART TO STAY SOBER

Humility "I've never seen anybody who's too dumb to stay sober. But I've met a few people who were too smart!" These wise words by an older member sum up what we sometimes see—people who feel turned off by the program because it seems too simple and involves so many people of ordinary education and backgrounds.

Alcoholism is much like other diseases in the way it strikes all people. Diabetes, for example, victimizes people of all intelligence and educational levels. We could never believe that being smart would give us an advantage in dealing with such an illness.

In the same way, the very smart person has no edge over others in gaining sobriety. In fact, pride in such gifts can be a stumbling block. It can be a barrier to the simple acceptance and surrender needed for success in the Twelve Step program.

We do have many very smart people in AA. They are also wise enough to know that nobody can outsmart John Barleycorn.

We can feel grateful for mental abilities and education that help us get along in the world. Our sobriety, however, is a separate type of gift that we did not create.

NOVEMBER 23

THE ONLY REASON TO DRINK

Staying Sober "There's only one real reason I can ever have for taking a drink, and that's because I want to."

This remark at a meeting sums up AA's position on why we drink. We never really drink because of pressures and troubles. We drink because we want to, because we feel like taking a drink.

It's true that a serious crisis, like going into bankruptcy, may make us conscious of an urge to drink. But we know that we're also likely to have such urges in the face of good fortune. The alcoholic who would drink over a bankruptcy would also probably get drunk if he or she won the lottery.

By refusing to accept all of these alleged "reasons" for drinking, AA simplified our problem so we can deal with it. We either want to drink or we don't want to drink, period. Even if we want to drink—and some members do—AA can show us how to stay sober and eventually lose such desires.

Nothing has the power to make me drink today. It is only my own willfulness that can destroy my sobriety.

NOVEMBER 24

ARE THERE BETTER
PATHS TO SOBRIETY?

Self-Honesty Now that alcoholism recovery has been well established, alternatives to the AA program are being developed. These are designed to appeal to those who either will not or cannot accept AA.

Nobody in AA should feel threatened by these new programs. We should, in fact, be delighted if ways are found to reach those whom we are unable to help. The need is so great that we should welcome anything that helps alcoholics.

The only real test for any program is that it works. More important, it must work for us. No program is useful to us if we cannot apply it in our own lives.

If we have found sobriety in AA, we have no need to look further. If AA was able to help us in our hour of desperate need, it can help us as the days unfold into the future.

I'll be thankful today for the sobriety AA has given me. I'll also remember that my need for help in maintaining sobriety will never end.

NOVEMBER 25

WHAT OUGHT TO WORK—
BUT DOESN'T

Understanding Alcoholism One of the old theories about alcoholism was that we drink because we had deep psychological problems. It followed that if we could clear up these problems, we would no longer need to drink excessively.

Another theory was that staying dry for a long period of time would dislodge one's alcoholic tendencies. After a certain length of sobriety, we would be able to return to normal drinking.

Both theories sound plausible, but in practice neither has worked. Many of us came to grief trying to make these ideas work.

What we eventually learn about psychological problems is that they may intensify our troubles, but they are not the real cause of our alcoholism. The cause may be rooted in some physical problem that enables us to achieve unusual highs from drinking. We also know that one drink acts as a trigger for more drinking—at least for us.

Our answer has been, first and foremost, to eliminate the first drink. Even if it doesn't square with theories, it works.

No matter how long I've been sober, one drink would be deadly to me. Accepting that fact enabled me to get sober after finding that theories about my problem weren't working.

NOVEMBER 26

ADMITTING POWERLESSNESS

Admission   If "admitting powerlessness" is still irritating to some of us, we're not alone. This aspect of AA is even criticized at times. It sounds to some like an unnecessary admission of weakness.

But we often admit powerlessness in other situations. We call the doctor because we are powerless to provide our own treatment. We seek advice and help on other matters. Why is it so bad to admit that we're powerless over alcohol?

Our trouble with this admission may be caused by false ideas about the nature of alcoholism. We may still feel that our wholeness as people somehow is wrapped up in an ability to drink in moderate amounts. Being able to "hold our liquor" or drink socially may still hold some importance for us.

As soon as possible we need to rid ourselves of these false ideas. Admitting powerlessness in AA is not an admission of total weakness. It is actually the key to finding real power and purpose, perhaps for the first time in our lives.

Since I've admitted powerlessness over alcohol, I've found new powers and opportunities in following the program. As a result, I'll remember that I'm a more effective person.

NOBODY OD'S ON AA

Balance Do people really need daily AA meetings, perhaps even two or three a day? Frequent meeting attendance is usually considered beneficial in AA, but nonmembers may frown on the practice, especially if a person is neglecting other responsibilities in the meantime.

One thing to remember is that nobody can really "OD" on AA. The worst that can happen from attending so many meetings would be eventual boredom from too much of the same thing. But no harm can come from too much of what is essentially a good practice.

If a person is attending lots of meetings, this schedule may eventually be cut back to allow time for other activities. It's better, especially in early recovery, to attend too many meetings than too few. We also have to let each person decide how many meetings are required at any stage in his or her recovery.

I know that everyone needs a balanced life, but that cannot happen without secure recovery. Meetings are my best way of staying active in the fellowship.

SPACES IN TOGETHERNESS

Friendship   One of the beautiful aspects of AA is the bonding that develops among members. We truly do achieve a closeness with some people that is unlike anything we ever had before.

The danger in such friendships is that we may become too close in some ways. Without realizing it, we may be making too many demands on others' time. This can become suffocating to them and eventually detrimental to the friendship.

In such situations, we need to remember the words of Kahlil Gibran: "Let there be spaces in your togetherness." However close we feel to others, we must allow them their space.

We should also remember to respect others' privacy as well as their anonymity. AA should give us close friendships, but not to the point of suffocation.

I'll remember today not to overstep my boundaries in any friendship. There must be spaces in our togetherness.

NONE ARE OBLIGATED TO US

Service Service is considered an essential part of AA. As Dr. Bob said, AA is really love and service.

If this service is delivered in the right spirit—the true AA spirit—no sense of obligation is created. If others feel they are incurring an obligation, they will resent us in time. Moreover, our carrying of the message will be flawed.

The proper way to look at service is to see it as something we perform for our own benefit. While we hope that it will benefit others, that does not have to happen in order for us to benefit. Our good comes from the giving of service, not the measurement of its results for others. No one is obligated to us; nor does anyone have the right to complain if our services did not help. We serve entirely for our own benefit.

For my own good, I'll give service today. I want it to be effective for others, but I realize my real purpose is to help myself.

NOVEMBER 30

SPIRITUAL PRIDE

Seeking Humility Those of us who have found a Higher Power in our lives can feel truly blessed. We know we're on the right path by witnessing the wonderful changes that continue to come into our lives.

One pitfall in this, however, is the risk of becoming "spiritually proud." We sometimes feel that our beliefs are so superior that others should accept them as well. We even become critical of the beliefs of others.

If this happens, we actually will be severing our own conscious contact with our Higher Power. False pride in a new form will be back in charge. Others will sense this too, and may withdraw from us.

Our best safeguard against this trap of spiritual pride is a reminder that we don't have all the answers. We can share our understanding with others, but we should never imply that we know what's best for them. Spiritual growth should bring humility, not more of the pride that was destroying us.

I can leave all outcomes in God's hands today, knowing that everything is being controlled in a spiritual way.

December

DECEMBER 1

WHY DO BAD THINGS HAPPEN?

Understanding Life   No one has been able to explain why pain and misfortune must be part of the human condition. Bad things can and do happen to everybody, and sometimes there's no way to explain it.

Even in sobriety, AA members have misfortunes—times when it appears that God is hiding. We even hear members share such experiences at meetings.

Many of us have found ways to use misfortunes constructively, however, by seeing how the program helps us deal with it. In some cases—but not all—we even learn that a misfortune was a disguised blessing.

Most important, by using the program, we are eliminating the drinking that has been the cause of many misfortunes in our lives. That alone makes our immediate world a much better place for everyone.

My life today can be both easy and hard. It gives me great comfort to know that I am not making conditions worse for myself and others.

DECEMBER 2

BRINGING PROJECTS TO COMPLETION

Fortitude Starting projects without completing them can be part of our alcoholic nature. It's related to immaturity and a tendency to become bored and discouraged quickly.

The Twelve Step program can help us overcome this problem. First, we realize and admit to such tendencies, fearlessly facing what has really been a very bad habit. Then we become honest about our motives. We realize that we didn't actually have the abiding interest that would have helped us complete some projects. In such cases, the projects never should have been started—and in the future we'll take care not to embark on similar projects.

When something does need to be completed, the program will help us stay with it until it's done. We will always find that the satisfaction of completing a necessary project will be part of sober living. We'll also know that we're growing in the program.

I'll take the necessary steps today to move any project toward completion. This will also help with future projects.

DECEMBER 3

RAISING THE FRUSTRATION THRESHOLD

Achievement What happens when we hit snags in our lives? In drinking, it was a common practice to chuck everything and just get drunk. This always made things worse, sometimes so much so that we forgot about the problem that triggered our frustrations.

Dealing with frustration is another part of growing up emotionally. Self-understanding in sobriety will help us detect surges of anger and irritation when things aren't going as planned. We'll recognize these feelings as being the same emotions that plagued us in our drinking days.

In sobriety, however, we are given choices. We actually do have the choice of pausing, letting the anger drain away, and then taking charge of the situation by knowing that God is working along with us. By doing this, we can eventually raise our threshold of frustration.

If some task or issue makes me angry today, I'll back off and place the outcome in God's hands. I'll know this is working when I have a change in feeling about it.

DECEMBER 4

THE LURE OF GREENER PASTURES

Gratitude   One of our old-timers spent a great deal of time trying to find a new job but never succeeding. When he finally retired, on a good pension, it became clear that the job he had kept was probably better and provided more benefits than any job he had been seeking. He was fortunate that none of his proposed job searches ever worked out.

The fantasy of finding "greener pastures" is something many of us face, in both drinking and sobriety. We may be very well off where we are, yet feel that something rich and exciting is over in the next meadow. We can feel this way about our jobs, our lifestyles, and our locations.

The answer to this greener-pastures obsession is to feel more gratitude for what we have here and now. We might also focus more upon today's activities and less upon impossible dreams of other places.

There may be greener pastures somewhere, but I'll first look for the opportunities and benefits of my own life and surroundings. I may be richly blessed without knowing it.

DECEMBER 5

HOLDING HANDS AND HUGGING

Sincerity The custom of holding hands while saying the Lord's Prayer has been adopted by many AA groups. We have also seen more hugging than in the past, even between the most unlikely members.

Are these new practices good or bad? In accordance with AA tradition, we have to leave such questions to the group conscience.

One thought, however, is that such physical actions do not necessarily mean that any true spiritual bonding has taken place. The old-timers who never held hands or hugged still had a great closeness in spirit and in feeling.

We must also consider that we may be violating the privacy of the person who doesn't wish to hold hands or hug. If such a person chooses to stand outside the hand-holding circle, he or she may be cast in the role of dissenter. Would this be fair?

Hand-holding and hugging may be here to stay, but let's not make them out to be more than mere physical expressions. The program of the heart is still first.

I'll remember today that true bonding is spiritual, not physical.

DECEMBER 6

ALCOHOLISM:
DISEASE OR BAD HABIT?

Understanding My Problem While AA has always considered alcoholism a disease, controversy still simmers over its definition. In the past, alcoholism has been considered a sin, a sickness, or just a very bad habit. More recently, there has been a suggestion that some "problem drinkers" might not be alcoholics at all and can very possibly bring their drinking under control.

This controversy will undoubtedly continue, but it is important that recovering people understand the *nature* of alcoholism. It is deadly, it is compulsive, and it is progressive. While there are occasional reports of alcoholics who claim to have become controlled drinkers, few of us have any firsthand evidence of such changes. Much more often, we hear the stories of alcoholics who try to drink again, only to find themselves headed down a rocky road.

It is not necessary that we define alcoholism perfectly or precisely. What's more important is that we remember we're powerless over alcohol and cannot safely pick up a drink. No definition will change that reality for an alcoholic who has had an unmanageable life.

I'm fortunate AA gave me an understanding of my problem that I can live with—one that will help me continue living. Others can worry about defining alcoholism. I'll focus on staying sober myself.

WHAT RATHER THAN WHO

Principles before Personalities   We're sometimes led to do something because a persuasive or important person recommends it. This is, in fact, the strategy behind endorsement advertising.

We learn in AA that it's more important to ask *what* is right rather than *who* is offering a course of action. If a course of action is right, it matters not who recommends it. If it is wrong, a dozen important people cannot make it right by endorsing it.

There are, indeed, many important people whom we can know and trust. But we should always remember that every human being will turn out to have clay feet if he or she is set up as a god. Our trust must always be in our Higher Power and in principles that never fail.

I'll not be unduly impressed today by persuasive, charismatic people. I'll follow their ideas only if I believe them to be right. Principles have a precedence over personality.

DECEMBER 8

A NEW FRAME OF MIND

Mood Control   Long after AA was started, the term *mood-altering drug* came into vogue. Though this originally was applied to hard drugs, it is also true of alcohol.

There's nothing wrong with wanting to alter one's mood. None of us really wants to be depressed, anxious, or fearful. We're all looking for ways to stay happy and high-spirited.

The problem with all mood-altering drugs, alcohol included, is that they provide temporary highs while bringing on long-term destruction and enslavement. We would love to have those highs if they did not carry such a terrible price.

But we can seek a new frame of mind in sober living that will give us better moods without destroying us. This is "the peace that passes all understanding," and it comes only from living the right way and listening to our Higher Power. This is the only mood control that really works.

I want to be in a good mood today, but it must be as a result of having a healthy frame of mind. I have no desire for the false highs that were killing me.

FIXING THINGS THAT AREN'T BROKEN

Self-Acceptance   At the beginning of our AA sobriety, we were reminded that we were not reformers. Yet we sometimes have a tendency to want to "reform" ourselves or others after we've established sobriety.

This can become a practice of "fixing things that aren't broken." We may not realize it, but many things in our lives and personalities were always all right, all along. In believing that we should be changed, we may be taking on the opinions of someone else. There might be no need for change at all.

We also may be trying to please people who disapproved of us. Perhaps we're trying to obtain the affection of a parent who always rejected us. But if we're already on a spiritual path and are living rightly, there's no need for change. We'd be trying to fix something that isn't broken.

I'll accept myself and others as we are today. We are not out to reform anyone, including ourselves.

DECEMBER 10

HOW IMPORTANT IS IT?

Good Judgment All of our lives, many of us had to deal with "tempests in a teapot." These were minor problems that we somehow magnified until they became disasters.

Some of us also took refuge in the bottle when faced with problems. Remembering this with some guilt, we may feel a responsibility today to deal with every problem efficiently and promptly. This feeling might also create unnecessary anxiety. We can easily get to the heart of such matters by asking ourselves, "How important is it?" We might be making something far more important than it really is.

The importance of problems is revealed by our inability to remember what was upsetting us a week ago. Asking "How important is it?" can be a useful test to avoid excessive worrying about any problem.

I'll take a responsible attitude today, but I'll watch myself for a tendency to go to pieces over things that really aren't important in the long run.

KEEP THE FOCUS ON
PERSONAL RESPONSIBILITY

Responsible Attitudes Alcoholics often try to shift responsibility to others. We once thought it was possible to blame others for our drinking, and we had sneaky ways of manipulating family members so they would feel guilty and comply with our demands.

In sober living, we must not allow ourselves to slip back into this mode of thinking. Keeping the focus on personal responsibility is our best way of approaching all problems. "What is my responsibility in this?" is a good question to ask in evaluating our part in situations.

We are always responsible for our own sobriety. Beyond that, we're also responsible for maintaining good attitudes and making sure that our own anger and pride do not make any situation worse than it already is.

I'll be responsible today for my own thoughts, feelings, and actions. If any stressful issue or situation arises, I'll keep my focus on personal responsibility.

DECEMBER 12

DEMANDING CREDIT

Approval   The struggle for recognition sometimes takes an ugly form in AA. Even the pioneers of AA had disputes about who deserved credit for the fellowship's success.

Demanding credit and recognition is a loser's game for people who are seeking growth in sobriety. It is an indication that we still need applause and approval of the sort that drove us while we were drinking. It is a way of saying that we still don't believe good work should be done for its own sake, but rather for the applause that goes with it.

The real kicker is that people who demand recognition never get enough of it. Ironically, if we don't try to obtain credit for our actions, it sometimes comes anyway, without effort on our part.

I'll watch myself for any tendency to demand credit for the things I do in the program. My healthy growth in sobriety should be reward enough.

DECEMBER 13

VISUALIZING SUCCESS

Optimistic Thinking   Some people insist that we must visualize ourselves enjoying success if we ever hope to achieve it. AA says virtually the same about sobriety; in fact, "A Vision for You" is the name of a chapter in *Alcoholics Anonymous.*

There is a lot of talk in AA about projecting into the future and "seeing the worst." It takes far less energy—and it's far more constructive—to see our· selves doing our best, in sobriety and in all things

We have rich imaginative powers. Quite often, we used these gifts wrongly when we were drinking—we would create dark pictures of our future troubles, particularly in the depressed periods between drinking bouts.

In AA, we learn to use those same powers to see ourselves enjoying happy sobriety as well as a secure place in the world.

I'm confident that I'm growing in sobriety and building healthy relationships in all of my activities.

DECEMBER 14

THE BEST OF THE PAST

Living Today   We're told that we should forget the past when we come into AA. Since we can't change it, we should not waste time and energy reliving it.

Let's be careful, however, not to take this advice too literally. There was much in our past that was good, even when we were drinking. We have a right and a need to treasure these important things.

The real dangers of living in the past come either from brooding about its mistakes or from thinking that our best days are already behind us. We can think of the past as a foundation for the good we expect today and in all the days ahead.

I'll preserve the best in my memories of the past, knowing that these helped bring me to my present state of recovery.

WATCHING OUR BOUNDARIES

Personal Relationships Setting boundaries in personal relationships is how we manage actions that could otherwise get out of control. One firm boundary in AA, for example, is maintaining other members' anonymity, as well as our own. We are always overstepping boundaries if we disclose another's AA membership without permission.

It's wise, too, not to expect the easy familiarity of the meetings to carry over into all other activities. One member who was employed by another AA member apparently wondered why his boss was so easygoing and cordial at AA meetings and so remote and businesslike in the factory. It made perfect sense, however; their relationship in the plant was different from their AA relationship and required another set of boundaries.

We can protect ourselves and others by being careful to establish proper boundaries for all relationships. This means that what's appropriate for one setting may not be for another.

I'll check to be sure that I'm observing proper boundaries, for myself and others. I must not violate others' rights any more than I want my own violated.

DECEMBER 16

OTHERS MUST NOT DEFINE US

Self-Image   The thoughtless practice of lumping people into categories can be destructive. Some of us still seethe with resentment over the roles we were given in our families while growing up. We realize that this way of being defined was a put-down.

As adults living sober, we must now make sure that we define ourselves in ways that contribute to our success and happiness. If others attempt to attach labels to us, we must not accept this—at least not in our own minds.

If others are attempting to define us in this way, we must always ask whether we've invited such labeling. Did our behavior somehow give them this impression? Did we mask our true feelings to present an image with which we don't really want to live? Whatever the answer, we must take charge of defining who we are and what we want to be.

If I don't like the way people have been viewing me, I'll change the signals I've been sending out. Any signals I send should fit the way I really want to be known.

LOOKING FOR PROTECTORS

Self-Reliance Many of us managed to survive while drinking by finding protectors we could lean on. Sometimes the protector wasn't a very strong person—only someone who was willing to support us in some way. A protector could even be a person who gave us flattery or companionship when we wanted it.

Such alliances are usually unhealthy and have no lasting place in sobriety. We cannot depend on protectors who will eventually betray us or fail us through no fault of their own.

In sobriety, we must grow into a satisfactory form of self-reliance. This is not reliance on our own resources; rather, it is really a way of relying on our Higher Power, the group, our sponsors, and the higher understanding we've found in the program. If we're still looking for people willing to protect us, we need more growth in sobriety.

I've been given tools for understanding myself and my life. I can use those tools effectively as I go through the day.

THE FEAR OF LONELINESS

Raising Self-Esteem The fear of being alone brings strange results. It may cause us to cling to arrangements and relationships that are unsatisfactory or destructive. Some of us become enablers for loved ones who are still drinking; quite often this can involve putting up with abuse we shouldn't have to endure.

We endure such relationships because we fear we'll be alone and defenseless without them. We may even put up with friends who are manipulative or treacherous because we can't visualize having happier, healthier friendships.

When we recognize that we are holding on to unsatisfactory relationships for such reasons, we need to apply the program more diligently in our own lives. Usually, we need more self-esteem—a belief that we deserve satisfactory relationships. We do not have to be alone, but neither do we have to endure what amounts to abuse and rejection.

Whether I'm with people or alone today, I'll know that all of my relationships should be satisfactory for everybody involved. I'll let my Higher Power guide me to the relationships that are right for me.

DEADLINES

Facing Delays The procrastination of our drinking years caused some of us to become compulsive and fearful about meeting deadlines. We fret and stew if we're unable to get things done when we think they should be completed.

Without being careless or irresponsible, we should remember that we're really living in a spiritual world on a spiritual basis. There are times when a delay even turns out to be beneficial because additional information or assistance turns up later on to ensure the success of a project.

It is part of mature living to keep promises and to meet the proper deadlines. Let's be sure, however, that we're not simply meeting unrealistic deadlines of our own making. We don't have to do this to atone for any failures of the past.

I'll look over my plans today to make sure that I haven't set any unrealistic deadlines for myself. I may be trying to do too much, too soon.

DECEMBER 20

RETURNING TO BASICS

Continuing   Now and then, an AA discussion focuses on the theme of "returning to the basics." This is a good time to shake out the excessive concerns that might be cluttering up our lives.

No matter how long we've been living in sobriety, we can never afford to dismiss the basic reasons we came to AA in the first place. We had made a mess of our lives, and no human power could relieve our alcoholism. By accepting and admitting this, we were able to find a new way of life.

This was also our admission ticket to the larger society, where people are concerned about many things. We sometimes become too caught up in all these concerns, even to the extent of forgetting our own needs. It's good, occasionally, to focus a meeting on AA basics. They are as essential today as they were when we first knew that we needed them.

I'll remind myself today that the basics give me a firm foundation on which to stand.

KEEPING THE FAITH WITH GUIDANCE

Good Orderly Direction Does guidance from our Higher Power always come through? We must believe that it does, even when we don't seem to receive a visible answer.

Spiritual guidance usually doesn't come as we think it should. What we're likely to find instead is that over time, a number of unrelated events come together for a good purpose. Although this appears to be chance or coincidence, very important outcomes often develop from simple happenings—maybe just from meeting someone on the street.

We can never really determine how any chain of events will play out. The best we can do is to continue seeking guidance while following the highest principles in our program. Many chance happenings will be recognized as guidance when we look back at an entire chain of events.

My best way to seek guidance is simply to remember today that my life and affairs are in God's care and keeping. The highest good will come from this.

DECEMBER 22

WATCHING WHAT WE THINK

Personal Inventory   It's healthy for AA members to confess personal difficulties with destructive thinking. When we find ourselves becoming too irritable or impatient, it's important to admit this in meetings or one-on-one discussions. Usually, just the admission of the problem helps solve it.

It's only false pride that makes us think we should be "above" destructive thinking. As human beings, we'll be susceptible to human failings no matter how long we've been sober.

If we continue to watch what we think, we'll also be able to head off very serious problems before they get out of control. Far from being a sign that we're not working the program, the practice of weeding out our current faults is the Tenth Step in action. Continuing to take personal inventory and admitting our wrongs is a safeguard against trouble.

Destructive thinking is no respecter of persons, and even as an older member, I could lapse into it today. I always have the Tenth Step, however, to get me back on track.

AA GOES THE DISTANCE

Fortitude Few societies or organizations have better ways of measuring success than AA. Since we are friends as well as recovering people, some of us get to know others fairly well over long periods of time. Even in a large city, we meet people again and again, year after year.

We've come to think it very commonplace that some individuals have been sober ten years or more, and that some members have been in the fellowship more than forty years.

The AA program does have staying power; it goes the distance for those who continue to follow it.

We should remind ourselves of this when we hear of new, faddish theories about alcoholism and recovery. Most of the time, the results reported are very short-term. What we really need is recovery with staying power, which we can find in the AA program.

Today's sobriety can be another link in an endless chain of sobriety. AA will go the distance for me if I take care of each day as it comes.

DECEMBER 24

JEALOUSY TOWARD LOVED ONES

Feeling Though resentment gets more attention in AA than jealousy, both of these ugly emotions can plague us in sobriety. Some of us can be very distressed and ashamed when the green demon of jealousy suddenly assaults us. Does this mean we're not working our program?

No, because the purpose of our program is to bring honesty and healing into our lives, not denial of basic human emotions. It's very understandable that we have pangs of jealousy even in sobriety. Quite often, this jealousy will be felt toward loved ones and close friends.

One young AA father discovered he was jealous of his wife when their infant son seemed more responsive to her than to him. We can also experience jealousy when others close to us receive things we'd like to have. It's even possible to be jealous of another's standing in AA.

When such feelings arise, we always have the answer: We must discuss our feelings with certain AA friends and turn these problems over to our Higher Power. This, not denial, is always the solution.

If the green demon of envy and jealousy arises today, I'll let the healing power of the Twelve Steps go to work on it.

DECEMBER 25

LIKING OURSELVES

Self-Esteem It's maybe unsettling to learn that we need to like ourselves more, especially when we've often been accused of being conceited.

Being conceited does not mean liking oneself; it's really a matter of being smug and contemptuous in our dealing with others. This attitude is easily recognized by others, and it causes them to dislike us.

However, if we like ourselves in the right way, others sense this too, and they will be drawn to us. We will truly like ourselves more as we learn to practice the principles of AA. We will like the kind of life we are trying to live. We will like ourselves for practicing fairness and honesty. We will also like ourselves for letting people see us as we are and feel comfortable doing so. In liking ourselves, we feel no need to impress or dazzle others.

I'll remember today that I have a right to be in the world. I will do my best to be fair toward others, but I will like myself regardless of their reactions.

HUMILITY:
TEACHABLE AND HONEST

Open to Growth *Humility* is often used in the context of being honest enough to admit one's faults, but it also means being teachable. The truly humble person realizes there's always more to learn and is open to such learning.

If we *think* we have humility, we usually don't. However, we can look back and recognize times when we made wonderful progress while being deeply humble. This was particularly true when we recognized our alcoholism and achieved sobriety. In this one action, we changed our lives.

If we continue to practice the honesty, open-mindedness, and willingness that helped get us sober, these traits will be apparent in other areas of our lives. Though humility isn't generally sought as a way of life, it's the right way for recovering people.

I'll be open today to ideas from any direction. I can learn something from every person.

LIMITING GOSSIP

No Harm to Others   "When you've told me their names, do not tell me their faults," a woman said at an AA meeting. She was explaining how careful we must be to keep gossip within tight limits. However, it is possible to identify people in gossip without actually speaking their names. We can give so many facts that the listener can identify whom we're discussing. This is no less malicious and thoughtless than actually naming the person.

We can avoid these dangers by giving up both the desire to gossip and the wish to listen to gossip. We will always have matters to gossip about; we can always find weaknesses in those we envy, faults in people we want to see taken down a notch or two. But if we persist in the program, we should find ourselves moving out of this limited way of thinking. We'll put severe limits on gossip at the same time.

I'll sidestep gossip if it starts to find a way into my life today. Under God's guidance, I have better things to do.

DECEMBER 28

REHEARSING REJECTION

Fortitude The possibility of rejection exists with almost everything we do, if we are free to choose. We might not like rejection, but we want the same freedom to reject others. As freely choosing people, we need to turn down ideas or proposals we don't like.

One thing we should never do, however, is rehearse rejections before they occur. If we do this, we may give up even before we have attempted what we hope to accomplish. In effect, we will be killing our hopes even before others have a chance to review them. This is always a ticket to failure.

Rejection is really a feedback mechanism that reports information we ought to have. It tells us either to change our approach or to seek acceptance elsewhere. It is not evidence that we're completely unacceptable.

Our problem with any single rejection may be that it causes us to recall all the rejections we ever had. We can learn to see any rejection as a normal event that can be beneficial if we accept it properly.

I'll not let any fear or visualization of rejection keep me from actions I ought to take today. I am an acceptable person, and there is a place for what I have to offer.

DECEMBER 29

MENDING THE PAST

No Regrets of the Past   "The past is best mended by living so fully today that its errors have no place in our lives." These words by an AA member suggest an approach for healing from the past.

All of us would benefit to use today's knowledge to deal with situations we mishandled in the past. But we must remember that whatever mistakes we made, we had available only the knowledge and resources we possessed then, and we may have done about as well as we possibly could at the time.

We should also remember that active alcoholism is a crippling and ugly disease with many terrible consequences. It's not surprising that bad things happened to us and to others when we were drinking. We can only be grateful that we are now recovering and that matters are better, not worse, than they once were.

I'll live fully today, allowing no thoughts of regret from my past to intrude.

MATURITY MEANS PRINCIPLES

Right Action   A principle is sometimes defined as a fundamental guide to action. The more mature we become, the more likely it is that we'll work from principles rather than blind feelings.

The principles outlined in the Twelve Steps are good guides for mature living. They call for honesty in motive, fair and considerate treatment of others, and reliance on our Higher Power throughout each day.

As we continue on such a path, we will outgrow the childish selfishness and reactions that were so destructive in our old lives. We will be viewed by others as mature, responsible, reliable people.

We also grow into maturity by acting according to sound principles even when we don't always feel like it. Whatever our feelings might be at any given moment, we can choose actions that are sound and constructive.

Whatever my feelings might be from moment to moment, I'll act according to the best principles today. I know this is a part of growing up.

HAS IT BEEN A YEAR OF GROWTH?

Growth   As any year draws to a close, we should reflect on how we have grown in sobriety. We should also identify changes during the year that enabled us to overcome bad habits and to move closer to better patterns of living.

Though we never are guaranteed favorable outcomes, we should always remember that sobriety is its own best reward. We want a full life of course, but it must begin with a decision to seek and to maintain sobriety at all costs.

We find that with sobriety, lots of other problems seem to solve themselves. Even if they don't, we have the tools to move forward and to achieve goals that always eluded us while we were drinking. Every year in sobriety is a year of growth.

I'll be conscious today of recent improvements I've made in my life and all my affairs. With sobriety, these improvements will go on for a lifetime.

INDEX

W

Other titles that will interest you . . .

Each Day a New Beginning

Daily Meditations for Women

The first daily meditation guide created by and for women involved in Twelve Step recovery programs. Hundreds of thousands of women have found help in this collection of thoughts and reflections that offer hope, strength, and guidance every day of the year. 400 pp.
Order No. 1076

Day by Day Second Edition

Daily Meditations for Addicts

These inspirational daily meditations add to and reinforce N.A. principles for living drug-free as they help us consider both the complexities of today's world and the simplicity of the Twelve Step program. 400 pp.
Order No. 1099

Touchstones

Daily Meditations for Men

This daily meditation book offers a rare blend of inspiration and support for any man involved in a Twelve Step recovery program as he explores new pathways in his life. 400 pp.
Order No. 5029

For price and order information, or a free catalog, please call our Telephone Representatives.

HAZELDEN

1-800-328-9000	1-651-213-4000	1-651-213-4590
(Toll-Free U.S., Canada, and the Virgin Islands)	(Outside the U.S. and Canada)	(FAX)

Pleasant Valley Road • P.O. Box 176 • Center City, MN 55012-0176
hazelden.org